"*Lost at 15, Found at 50* has the [...] that has seen the author move [...] for travel and work and the re[...] as enriching as it is illuminati[...]

Yale-NUS College, Singapore

"Combining her life-time experiences, journalistic skills and talent for story-telling, Ashwini has brought forth a wonderful book. It should appeal to readers of all ages."
— K. Kesavapany, Governor, Singapore International Foundation

"*Lost at 15, Found at 50* is a rollercoaster of a memoir that takes you racing through time and space, starting with India still in its teens, to an icy, post-Khrushchev Moscow, to a Washington under siege, to a Sikkim in turmoil, to Burma, to South Korea. Don't miss the ride. It will leave you breathless – and asking for more."
— Kiran Doshi, author of *Jinnah Often Came to Our House*

"Ashwini is a talented story-teller and this book is a wonderful, gripping book, that everyone, especially women, should read. It's a travelogue, a lesson in history and a life manual all in one. I highly recommend this book."
— Ira Trivedi, author and yoga master

"A personal testimony of wandering through the lanes and bylanes of the late twentieth and early twenty-first century history. This is not a history of great world events – that is in the backdrop – but of what it was really like to live through those times."
— Sanjeev Sanyal, author and economist

"Ashwini Devare represents India's post-midnight generation – born not in the flush of the freedom that arrived on the midnight of August 15, 1947 but within the cohort that appeared between the searing defeat in the China war of 1962 and the massive victory over Pakistan in 1971 that stamped New Delhi's dominance over the sub-continent. Daughter of a distinguished Indian Foreign Service officer, Ashwini Devare has written a memoir that also tells her father's story: the Indian external relations journey starting with the nervously uneasy proximity with the Soviet Union, the instinctively warm but ideologically distant United States, hegemonic behaviour in Sikkim and the easy moorings India found in Singapore as the springboard of the contemporaneous Look East/Act East policy."

– Ravi Velloor, Associate Editor and Asia columnist,
*The Straits Times*

"A fresh and lively narrative, suffused with the authenticity of a bright-eyed child growing into adulthood from her front-row seat to world-changing international events. Ashwini Devare's memoir makes you homesick for places you've never set foot, all the while giving you a glance into the often not-so-glamorous life of an Indian diplomat and his family. More than anything, the book demonstrates how seemingly distant political incidents shape the lives of individuals, both natives and those who are temporary guests in a foreign land."

– Anne Ostby, author of *Pieces of Happiness*

*A Memoir*

# Lost at 15, Found at 50

**Ashwini Devare**

Travel, trials & tribulations
in foreign lands

© 2019 Marshall Cavendish International (Asia) Private Limited
Text © Ashwini Devare

Published by Marshall Cavendish Editions
An imprint of Marshall Cavendish International

All rights reserved

No part of this publication may be reproduced, stored in a retrieval system or transmitted, in any form or by any means, electronic, mechanical, photocopying, recording or otherwise, without the prior permission of the copyright owner. Requests for permission should be addressed to the Publisher, Marshall Cavendish International (Asia) Private Limited, 1 New Industrial Road, Singapore 536196. Tel: (65) 6213 9300. E-mail: genref@sg.marshallcavendish.com
Website: www.marshallcavendish.com/genref

The publisher makes no representation or warranties with respect to the contents of this book, and specifically disclaims any implied warranties or merchantability or fitness for any particular purpose, and shall in no event be liable for any loss of profit or any other commercial damage, including but not limited to special, incidental, consequential, or other damages.

Other Marshall Cavendish Offices
Marshall Cavendish Corporation. 99 White Plains Road, Tarrytown NY 10591-9001, USA • Marshall Cavendish International (Thailand) Co Ltd. 253 Asoke, 12th Flr, Sukhumvit 21 Road, Klongtoey Nua, Wattana, Bangkok 10110, Thailand • Marshall Cavendish (Malaysia) Sdn Bhd, Times Subang, Lot 46, Subang Hi-Tech Industrial Park, Batu Tiga, 40000 Shah Alam, Selangor Darul Ehsan, Malaysia

Marshall Cavendish is a registered trademark of Times Publishing Limited

**National Library Board, Singapore Cataloguing-in-Publication Data**

Names: Devare, Ashwini.
Title: Lost at 15, found at 50 : a memoir : travel, trials and tribulations in foreign lands / Ashwini Devare.
Description: Singapore : Marshall Cavendish Editions, [2019]
Identifiers: OCN 1052723708 | ISBN 978-981-4828-82-6 (paperback) Subjects:
LCSH: Devare, Ashwini. | Women, East Indian--Travel--Biography.
Classification: DDC 305.48891411092--dc23

Printed in Singapore

In this memoir, names, places and experiences are based on the author's memories, conversations and recollections. Some of the dialogues, names and scenes have been changed or recreated to protect individual privacy. Any resemblance to actual persons, living or dead, is purely coincidental.

*For Mom, Dad and Aparna*

## Contents

**Behind the Iron Curtain**     9
Russia *1965–1967*

**The Other Side of the Cold War**     37
USA *1967–1970*

**Kingdom of Hope**     61
Sikkim *1970–1974*

**Brown Girl in the Ring**     83
Switzerland *1976–1979*

**Behind the Bamboo Curtain**     113
Burma *1979–1981*

**Feels Like Home**     131
India *1981–1985*

**The Land of the Morning Calm**     151
South Korea *1986–1989*

**Guns and Graffiti**     185
USA *1990s*

**Island in the Rain**     221
Singapore *2000s*

**Acknowledgements**     255

**About the Author**     256

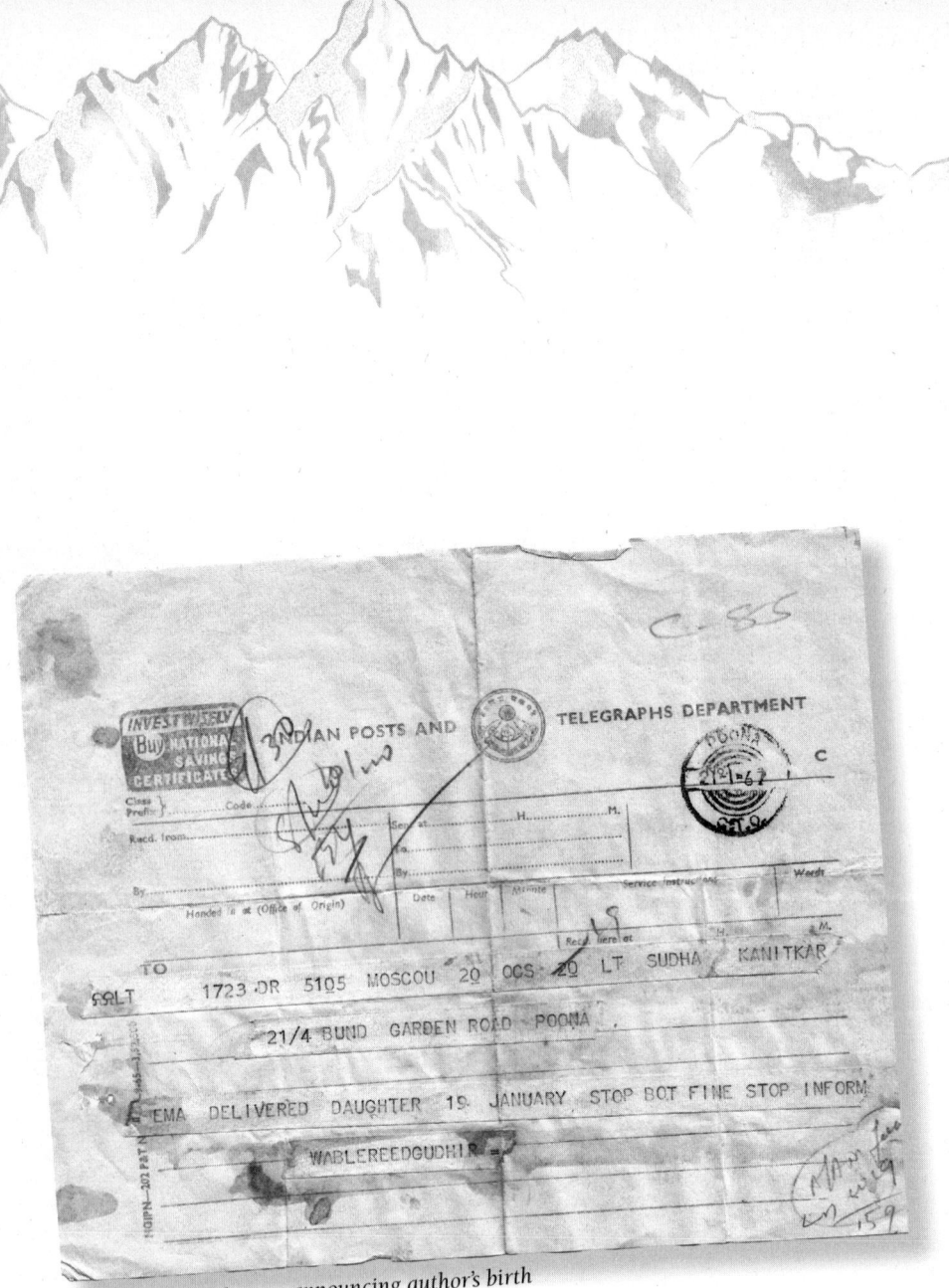

Telegram from Moscow announcing author's birth

# Behind the Iron Curtain

**RUSSIA**
*1965–1967*

## Moscow

A slender young woman stood at the hospital window, straining her eyes through the sleet that buffeted the street six floors below. My mother clutched me tightly in her arms, her child-like face pinched with fatigue and anxiety, eager eyes searching the sidewalk corner where she knew her husband would be waiting to catch a glimpse of his young wife and newborn.

Snow fell steadily, casting a silver metallic over the darkening afternoon. Suddenly my mother spotted him in a swirl of snowflakes, huddled in a coat, scarf and a hat, bracing one of the bitterest January days of the year. She waved wildly, her face brightening the minute his outline emerged through the snow.

"Look, there's Daddy!" She lifted me higher in the hope that he could see us: two blurry little dots outlined against a frosted steel window. Her eyes filled with tears, worrying about her husband shivering in his coat. He stood there, waving at us for a long while till the darkness swallowed him from sight.

My life began here, in the heart of Moscow, in a hospital for foreigners, near the grand Kropotkinskaya Station. There was nothing grand about the hospital though; it was stark and spartan, as were most institutions in communist Russia in those days. The austere maternity ward my mother and I were in was devoid of any toys or colours heralding the presence of a newborn; instead it had grey curtains and sheets, metal beds, steel trays and windows with grills. The week I was born coincided with a flu outbreak in the city and to seal off all infections, the hospital authorities immediately slapped draconian quarantine measures across all wards, forbidding visitors – even family members – from seeing patients. As a result of this sweeping ban, I did not get to see my father for the first fortnight of my life, except for those rare snatches of him standing on the roadside from our perch high above.

My birth created quite a stir at the hospital; it was the first time Russian nurses had seen a brown-skinned baby with dark hair. In fact, 'the girl with black hair' became a talking point in our ward and nurses from different departments came to peer at me and marvel at my jet-black halo of curls.

Just twenty years old, my mother was lonely and homesick, and welcomed the diversion. It helped her get through the long dreary days of being the lone Indian in the hospital, the agony of mastitis, and the postpartum depression that was washing over her in big giant waves.

"No, please, I cannot eat this," she shook her head at the plate of food the nurse had wheeled into the hospital room. She shut her eyes tightly to hide angry tears; this was the third day in a row she was being offered boiled potatoes and cabbage. Earlier, the nurse had brought in a juicy chicken drumstick which my mother refused, being a strict vegetarian. Fresh vegetables and fruits were in short supply in the streets of communist Moscow and, in any case, no one seemed to comprehend her desperate requests in broken Russian that she was a pure vegetarian, who did not even eat egg. As each day passed, my mother started becoming weaker. The pain of mastitis became unbearable and she stopped producing milk. It was only when a senior nurse noticed the untouched food trays leaving my mother's room that there was a sudden bustle of activity in our ward and senior staff were notified. The management then reluctantly agreed to my father's request to send in home-cooked food. From then onwards, every day, a 'tiffin' would arrive at the maternity ward, concealing within it the aromas of curry, vegetable and *chapati*, all of which deliciously boosted my mother's spirits for the rest of our hospital stay.

I loved Russian milk, which I drank in copious quantities the first year of my life. My father would go to one of the several 'milk kitchens' located near our house and buy small bottles of milk and yogurt, a common source of dairy for children in Moscow back then. My parents often joke about how the Russian milk made me bonny and strong, giving me good immunity in those early months.

"You never got sick," my mother told me. "It was definitely the Russian milk!"

---

"Ten days after your father and I tied the knot, we were off," my mother recalled. "The journey to Moscow was like the voyage of Sinbad, full of adventure. It was like going on a treasure hunt."

It was a story my sister and I would often curl up on the sofa to listen: my parents' foreign odyssey just a month after their marriage, which catapulted them from the confines of their small town Pune in India into the heart of communist Russia.

Defying all the predictions of the family astrologer that she would become a teacher, my mother had rushed to the altar instead, marrying a complete stranger who would whisk her off to the unknown. This stranger was Ravi, a thin, gawky Indian Foreign Service probationer, who had never stepped outside his home state of Maharashtra until he cleared the prestigious all-

India Civil Services Examination, which landed him in the capital, Delhi. A year later, Ravi's life would change dramatically when a senior bureaucrat in the Ministry of External Affairs (MEA) informed him that his maiden posting had been confirmed. "Young man, you have a month to get going," the officer told him sternly. "To Moscow."

Growing up, my father had always dreamed of faraway, distant lands, despite his small-town upbringing. The oldest of three children, he grew up on the campus of Pune's Wadia College where my grandfather was a professor. Wadia College was an institution that even back then attracted foreign students from countries as far away as the Middle East and Africa. Their house became a convening ground for intellectuals, students, writers and poets. These early influences would ultimately shape my father's curiosity about the bigger world that lay beyond the fringes of his hometown.

The year my father turned fourteen, my grandfather died unexpectedly, devastating his wife and three young children. In a single brutal blow, they were rendered penniless and homeless. They were forced to vacate their modest but comfortable accommodation on campus. Over the years my grandparents had nurtured deep friendships, and people whom they had helped along the way now stepped in, opening their homes to the shattered widow and her children. A trickle of money from the sales of my grandfather's academic books allowed the family to scrape through the next few years. My father and his sister put their heart and soul into their studies, sensing but not fully processing that education might be the only route for advancing their destinies.

My father applied to the school of engineering because that was what everyone around him did, but he realised very quickly it wasn't for him. His passion for political science kept bubbling, till it burst forth with a force that he could no longer ignore. My father had first heard about the Indian Foreign Service (IFS) through a friend. The civil services seemed like a nebula – floating mysteriously in a distant galaxy, out of reach for most ordinary middle-class Indians, many of whom had never heard of the IFS. My father was intrigued. He started to prepare for the Civil Services Examination with feverish gusto, studying engineering by day and political theory by night. The highly selective exam, once cleared, would open doors to the civil services, allowing candidates to choose their preference for the IFS, IAS (Indian Administrative Service) and other central services.

It could not have been an easy decision for my father; he was, after all, the oldest son. His sister was of marriageable age and his mother fretted about finding her a good family, a prospect that was daunting for a widow with meagre financial means. His brother, the youngest, was only ten and his future lay ahead, uncharted and uncertain. That he would be abandoning his family to vanish into the unknown, weighed heavily on my father's shoulders. With her characteristic pragmatism, his mother came to his rescue. She did not allow her own doubts to cloud what she predicted was a bigger, brighter canvas for her son. Hence, when it was time for my father to make his selection, he was able to choose the IFS freely, with full blessings from his mother.

The whirlwind began – beginning with boot camp at the Mussoorie Academy, a mandatory training requirement for all probationers in the civil services where they learned everything from horse riding to foreign languages. The choice of foreign language was decided by the MEA in Delhi and in my father's case, he was assigned Russian.

But there was a rather important matter that needed to be taken care of first. Just before he set off to Mussoorie, my father had experienced the first flutter of love. The subject of his fixation was a pretty young woman from the city of Nagpur, whose name had been suggested as an ideal match for my father by a common friend of both families. My paternal grandmother, eager to see her son married off before he left the shores of India, welcomed the solicitation enthusiastically.

Even though their marriage was 'arranged', my mother had already decided this was the man she wanted to marry. She had seen a black and white photograph of my father in a local newspaper that had published the list of IAS/IFS exam toppers – and immediately fallen in love. She saved the photograph and would look at it wistfully ever so often. The young man was not conventionally handsome, his face was thin and rather gaunt. His chin was a bit too pronounced and his demeanour, serious. But underneath that reserve, my mother sensed a man who was sensitive and good-natured. She was drawn to his eyes that looked gentle and kind.

As was customary in an arranged marriage, my father with half his family in tow arrived at my mother's house to 'see the bride'. In accordance with protocol, my mother had to serve all of them tea. She would tell us later how she hated going around with a tray, angry that my father had shown up with his entire family! Was he going to make a decision based on what *they* said? Did he not have a mind of his own? Yet, she couldn't be angry with my father for too long. Despite the presence of elders in the room, my parents had eyes only for each other and they knew instantly they would be soulmates.

The wedding was a hastened affair – a simple ceremony held

ten days prior to their departure to Moscow. For the couple that had to juggle two milestones simultaneously – marriage and a foreign posting – it was a frenzied fortnight of shopping for winter clothes, packing and goodbyes.

The day dawned for Ravi and my mother, Alka, to leave. Dozens of family members, some of whom had travelled overnight by bus, thronged the departure lounge at Bombay's Santa Cruz Airport. They came armed with food, flowers and affection, wanting to offer their blessings to the newlyweds. The couple stood amidst them, dazed, the blitzkrieg of the last few weeks clearly showing on their pale faces. My mother's side of the family were perplexed at the speed with which Alka had gone from chasing academic dreams to marrying a man who was taking her off to some faraway land. They eyed him suspiciously; a distant uncle openly wondered whether Ravi was a communist.

"My aunt Meena, she pressed my hands with so much love, she was not sure she would see me ever again," recalled my mother. "All my relatives had that look on their faces as if they thought this would be the last time they would see me."

Flying was a novelty in those days and the fact that someone in the family was headed off to a 'phoren' land, and on an airplane at that, was in itself a wondrous event that created quite a stir among relatives from both sides, many of whom had only heard of Moscow because of Raj Kapoor, the Indian mega star who brought Russia to the Indian public through his famous Bollywood blockbuster hit of the fifties, *Awaara*.

"What a commotion there was at the airport!" said my father.

"People came with bouquets and garlands, I felt like some sort of a politician," said my mother.

"We were carrying enormous amounts of luggage," said my

father. "We'd been told nothing was available in Moscow, so everyone brought all kinds of things for us to take along. And of course, your mother was carrying her famous *tanpura*." This stringed instrument that accompanied my mother's singing would journey with her throughout my father's postings.

"And all those woollen clothes," said my mother laughing. "I could only think of pictures of Eskimos and igloos from our geography books. We just grabbed whatever happened to be woollen – gloves, monkey caps, socks, scarves, underwear. We were haunted by tales of the Siberian winter, which we had heard caused exposed body parts like ears and noses to drop off! In Pune, our only contact with ice was ice cream. We had absolutely no inkling of the severity of winter in Moscow."

"After all, don't forget it was the Russian winter," said my father. "The famous winter that stopped the victorious advances of both Napoleon and Hitler."

In addition to their own luggage Ravi and Alka were carrying an assortment of items for the embassy staff in Moscow. "People had asked for things like toothpaste, *masalas*, even bananas and fresh coriander! They would wait longingly for someone to come from India, they were so deprived of consumer goods."

"We looked a real sight at the airport, your father and I. We were wearing our winter coats in the Bombay heat because we had no space in our luggage to put them! We stuffed full every pocket of our jackets and overcoats. We had handbags and *thaylas* (Indian cloth bags) on each shoulder, bursting at the seams with all sorts of things, and then we had these big garlands on top of the coats, from our loving relatives. I could barely be seen through all that!"

As their plane took off, my parents were acutely conscious that Air India represented the only link between their motherland

and a country that would become their new home. Because of the 1965 India-Pakistan war, flying over Pakistan was prohibited and as their aircraft detoured Iran, daylight dissolved into night, bringing them closer to the vast continent-like country of Russia. From the protected familiarity of their provincial lives, Ravi and Alka were suddenly catapulted into an utterly unknown world of foreign diplomacy that would become the vehicle for their globe-sprinting life across peregrine lands for the next forty years.

It was a pitch-black night. When the Air India flight began its descent, the blinking lights of Moscow appeared through the portholes and the drone of engines merged with the strains of sitar played in the aircraft PA system. As soon as my parents stepped out of the aircraft, soft flurries of snow landed on their cheeks and the young couple found themselves shivering in their grossly inadequate winter coats that had felt so snug and warm in Mumbai, but now suddenly felt like plastic.

"The whole area surrounding us at the tarmac was blanketed with snow, for a moment I thought I was in fairyland," said my mother.

With the raucous din of Mumbai still drumming in her ears, and the tears barely dry on her cheeks, she walked into the deserted silence at Sheremetyevo Moscow International Airport with a flutter of fear, and homesickness. India seemed light years away: the fading faces of her parents, bravely trying not to break down when she turned to wave at them one last time, her own face awash with tears as she walked out of the doors onto the tarmac, a light Bombay breeze gently swishing her hair, reassuring, whispering farewell.

Staring at the white people around her, my mother was uneasily reminded of the long distance from home. She turned to look at the man by her side who looked equally bewildered, but was fighting hard to maintain composure in front of his new wife.

They looked around for someone familiar and soon spotted the officer who was there to receive them. Ranjit Sharma rushed towards them, smiling and waving. Sharma was an old friend; my father and he had got to know each other well at the academy in Mussoorie. My mother felt instantly comforted to see a fellow Indian. Sharma was gregarious and warm, his enthusiasm the best antidote to their disorientation. He was delighted to have his old friend join him in Moscow and couldn't stop beaming.

"Welcome to Moscow, Ravi and Alka!" Sharma grinned, thumping my father vigorously on the back. Looking at their baggage spread out all around, he laughed, "*Arrey, yaar,* you've got the whole of India with you! I can't wait for my goodies!" Sharma suddenly spotted the *tanpura*. "I didn't realise we have a singer in our midst, wonderful, wonderful." And he slung the *tanpura* on his shoulder and rushed them through immigration. Brushing off their pleas of exhaustion, Sharma drove them straight to a party being hosted by an accountant friend of his, not even allowing them time to change first.

"We went with him in our bedraggled, dishevelled state," said my mother. "Someone at the party asked me whether I had any utensils and if I'd like to borrow some, and I had no idea what a utensil meant! I felt so out of place, so small-town, my clothes, accent, everything felt so inadequate. I was *so* embarrassed."

Ravi and Alka's initiation into the Foreign Service had officially begun.

The very next evening my parents were invited to dinner at the Indian Ambassador's residence. He was hosting a special meal to welcome the three new probationers, including my father.

"Do I have to go?" asked my mother in a meek voice. Shy and timid, the thought of dining with the Ambassador was a daunting prospect.

"We can't say no to the big boss, he's having the dinner to welcome us to the mission," said Ravi. "Don't worry, Sharma will be there. It's just him, Mehra and us." My mother knew of Mehra, the other probationer who worked in the embassy, but had yet to meet him.

The Indian Ambassador was a highly respected diplomat with powerful ties to the New Delhi political elite, handpicked by the Prime Minister's Office for Moscow, which was seen as a prized posting. New Delhi's top brass wanted a man in Moscow whom they could trust implicitly to secure India's interests with the Soviets. The Ambassador not only understood the Russians, he also knew the Americans well, having been posted to Washington prior to coming to Moscow. The Ambassador welcomed the couple warmly. Sharma and Mehra arrived at the same time, looking equally nervous. My father was the only married probationer among them, which seemed to accord him a slightly senior status among the bachelors.

"Please come in," said the Ambassador in his deep baritone, as he ushered them through the foyer into the living room, which looked imposing to the junior officers.

"I hope you are comfortable in your flats?" the Ambassador inquired courteously.

"Yes, Sir," answered all three in chorus.

The Ambassador looked at my mother. "Welcome to Moscow, young lady."

"Thank you," Alka stuttered, feeling acutely self-conscious.

The Ambassador felt a strong sense of responsibility towards the newly married couple, technically still on their honeymoon; and with his wife away in India, he was determined to make up for her absence with generous hospitality.

"Please, sit down, sit down."

My father had forgotten all about his wife, so preoccupied was he in making a good first impression on his boss. My mother sat down on the far end of a sofa, and looked around at the tastefully decorated living room, adorned with Indian paintings and objets d'art. A gleaming brass Ganesha figure sat in an alcove; a chandelier cast a luminous glow over the small group sitting awkwardly in front of the Ambassador. My mother shivered; despite the heating in the residence, her sweater and sari felt grossly thin.

"Ravi, I hope you've got your wife a warm coat, otherwise she can borrow my wife's," said the Ambassador.

"Yes, Sir, we have got coats, thank you, Sir," said my father.

"All right, then, what can I offer you gentlemen?"

Sharma asked for whisky, as did Mehra. At first my father hesitated, and then he too said, whisky. The Ambassador turned to my mother. "And what about you my dear girl? What would you like to have?"

My mother was tongue-tied and then, after a few seconds of silence, she blurted out, "Whisky."

There was a stunned silence. My father looked at her astonished. He was about to say something when the Ambassador, with a twinkle in his eye, said, "Have you had whisky before?"

"No," said my mother, mortified to have all eyes boring into her.

Still smiling, the Ambassador said, "Then I suggest you start with a glass of wine." He handed her a glass of wine, the colour of which seemed to match her flaming cheeks. She stared at the deep red liquid in her glass, and wondered how anything could taste so vile. The jet lag and homesickness were threatening to flood her any minute and she wanted to cry. Later that night when they were home, my father said, "Why did you ask for whisky?"

"Well, you said eating non-vegetarian food is compulsory in the Foreign Service, so I thought maybe drinking whisky is compulsory as well. That's why I asked for whisky."

For years afterwards, Sharma and Mehra would tease my mother about her love for hard liquor. It would be a long time before she was able to laugh with them without squirming when recounting her first official dinner at the Ambassador's.

---

My parents arrived in Moscow at the height of the Cold War, with Russia firmly entrenched behind the Iron Curtain. Every day was a reminder that this was deep communist territory. After almost a decade of being in power, in 1964, Nikita S Khrushchev was ousted from office by the triumvirate of his party comrades Alexei Kosygin, Leonid Brezhnev and N Podgorny who took over the reins of communist Russia. While Khrushchev had improved the standard of living for Russians and invested in the space programme, his reign was a turbulent one for the Soviet Union. In foreign policy, there had been dangerous developments, including the Cuban Missile Crisis in 1962 which brought the United States and the Soviet Union to the edge of war. Under the fresh leadership of the three men, a new dawn was rising over this mammoth country. Brezhnev would go on to sideline his rivals, consolidate power and rule the Soviet Union for the next two decades, building it into the world's superpower on a head-on collision with the United States.

In the wintry streets of Moscow there was a permanent pall of gloom, which weighed down the city like heavy old upholstery. The sun would rise at 9am, sometimes, never at all. No colour dared pierce the dreary landscape. The long, forbidding stretches of winter wrapped the city in a frigid, sunless grip. Life in the city was defined by constant shortages. Serpentine queues were intrinsic to everyday life in Moscow; from meat, milk and fruit to clothing, everything had to be stocked when it was available because once it disappeared from the shelves, no one could predict when the item would show up again. The exception to the dourness was ice cream, which the Russians simply loved. Rosy-cheeked children eating ice cream was a common sight in the city.

The spectre of the Second World War continued to haunt the Soviet Union, a country that had suffered the maximum loss of lives of nearly 20 million of its people. The regime would deliberately emphasise the sacrifices that had been made by the Russians in the war to evoke patriotic fervour and rationalise the hardships faced by the common people.

Ravi and Alka did not allow this doom to engulf them; instead they drank in their new environment in big gulps, like thirsty children. To them, fresh from India, Moscow felt grand and majestic. For the first few months, they were in a constant state of wide-eyed wonder. Together they discovered the romance of the Russian ballet as they watched *Swan Lake* at the Bolshoi

Theatre and soaked in the magic of the Russian Philharmonic Orchestra. They immersed themselves in *Voyna i Mir* (Tolstoy's *War and Peace*), a movie that had just been released in Russia. The melancholy of communist life could not crush Russia's long legacy of cultural richness in the arts, which bubbled softly under the veneer of austerity that marked day-to-day life in the city.

"I can never forget the first time I saw *Swan Lake*," said my mother. "When the orchestra began and the dancers came on stage, I couldn't tell if they were humans or swans, that's how graceful they were."

My father took a loan and bought a small Russian car, a bright red Moskvich. But there was one problem: he didn't know how to drive. Captain Kapoor, a senior defence officer at the embassy felt sorry for him and agreed to give him a few lessons. Every evening, for the next few weeks, Captain Kapoor would make my father practise up and down the embassy driveway till one evening he declared him fit to take his Moskvich on to the streets of Moscow. After that, there was no stopping my father, who would take his wife on long drives around the city. Together, they marvelled at the wide boulevards, the tree-lined avenues, the magnificent buildings and bridges arching the sky. They cruised along the Moskva River, through posh Arbat and Kalinin Prospekt, admiring the famous Hotel Ukraina, its Gothic spires illuminating the winter sky. They would drive up to the forested Lenin Hills and gaze down at the city below.

One area the communists had full mastery over was infrastructure. "Look," my father would point out to my mother. "They have special lanes for trams and trolley buses. And look at how wide the footpaths are." The subway that went deep into the bowels of the earth fascinated both of them. Many were ornate underground palaces, with chandeliers, marble statues and stained-glass murals, symbols of grandeur from the past. They observed how vestiges from Stalin's era were still stamped across much of the cityscape.

My parents enrolled in waltzing lessons. Once a week they would go for classes at Gorky Park, where they had a rare chance to interact with local Russians.

"We had to keep changing partners during the lesson," my mother recalled with a smile. "And every time a Russian girl would dance with Ravi, I'd get so jealous."

"She would sulk for days," chuckled my father, who had clearly enjoyed his lessons very much.

"Don't exaggerate. But yes, maybe for a few hours," acknowledged my mother, "that's because you never seemed to be in a hurry to go back home!"

---

Ravi and Alka's honeymoon period was short-lived. A year and a half later, I was born, on a cold blustery day in January when the chill dropped to minus thirty degrees Celsius and a wind blew across the frozen landscape. Snow had been falling for several days, leaving the city submerged in a deep freeze.

My mother had decided that if she were to have a girl, her daughter would have a Russian name. So she began to call me Irena. But when my grandmother, who continued to wield considerable influence even long-distance, was informed of my name, she was *not* pleased. Her grandchild, she declared, must be named after the first star in the Indian *nakshatra* (constellation) and Ashwini I became.

The days stretched out long and empty for my mother. Cooped up indoors with a fussy newborn became a punishing lesson in motherhood. From washing stashes of cloth diapers by hand and hanging them on the heater to dry, to looking for fresh ingredients for the baby's food and feeding and bathing the baby, to cooking for herself and her husband and cleaning up, days and nights became a blur of sleepless exhaustion. As days shortened and darkness enveloped their small apartment, she became terribly homesick. Visiting the local department stores left her feeling cheated because whenever she walked into the shop, the rows of empty shelves would be invariably devoid of toys, baby clothes, diapers and food.

It was my mother's innate positivity that allowed her to ward off potential depression in Moscow, a condition that was afflicting many, including some embassy officers' wives. They remained indoors, afraid of the cold, and became increasingly miserable. One of them would end her life in the months to follow, jumping off a high floor of an apartment building. Her suicide rattled the Indian community for months, especially my mother who had met the lady on numerous occasions at official functions.

My mother found that the best remedy for self-pity was to get outdoors. As soon as she saw the sun – on that rare occasion when it feebly peeked out – she would quickly bundle me in my pram and we'd head out to the small park near our house in Kutuzovskiy Prospekt. She was like a child excited by the newness of her surroundings; she wanted to share this new world with me. I became her constant companion, who adored her and wanted nothing but to see her dimpled smiling face above me, as she navigated my pram through the streets of our foreign home.

Sometimes she would take me to the Indian embassy. The

minute she walked into the foyer, she would forget the world outside. The tricolour fluttering in the foreground, officers chatting, children of staff members running about and the warmth of being in her comfort zone had no parallel; it was pure, unalloyed joy. All regional differences fell to the side, all Indian languages sounded comfortingly homely and everyone was united in one big bundle of solidarity.

"I was friendly with a Punjabi lady, I felt so close to her," said my mother. "Growing up in Pune, I'd never met a Punjabi before, and she too had never known a Maharashtrian. But we became best friends."

Fridays were especially busy at the embassy, when the weekly Air India flight would arrive with fresh vegetables and fruit, which would then be distributed among the staff.

"We would all gather to collect our vegetables, it was so exciting!" recalled my mother. "One of the officers would distribute the okras, the eggplant, spinach, pumpkin, coriander, while they were still fresh. I can still remember vividly how thrilled I was to make *palak paneer*."

The Embassy of India located in the heart of the city in Ulitsa Obukha was the nerve centre, playing a focal role in enhancing Indo-Soviet relations. Buzzing with delegations, official functions and parties, the embassy rarely had a lull. The imposing grey stone building, dating back to the eighteenth century, had once belonged to a Russian nobleman, which might explain its aristocratic flair. An outhouse in the embassy compound had a history that staffers would proudly narrate to visitors. During his victorious visit to Moscow, Napoleon had shown up at the main entrance of the embassy and tried to open the front door. When he couldn't, he ended up spending the night in the outhouse, which subsequently came to be known as Napoleon's Dacha.

Life in Moscow was like living in a giant aquarium with nowhere to hide. The Russian government scrupulously monitored the activities of all foreigners, including the diplomatic corps in Moscow. All foreigners, irrespective of their nationality, were seen as potential spies. My parents would tell us how they suspected that all our phones were tapped and rooms bugged, especially bedrooms! The dreaded four-letter word was the UPDK, the *Upravlenie Diplomatischaya Korpusa*, the government body which Lenin had started back in the 1920s to 'assist' foreigners. In reality, 'assistance' was a euphemism for surveillance because no one could keep out of the UPDK's octopus grip. That the KGB leaned heavily on the UPDK for information about foreign embassies in Moscow was well established.

"For every small thing we had to go through UPDK, that was the protocol," said my father. "Even the most basic administrative jobs had to be channelled through them. From fixing toilets to hiring maids, even if there was a cockroach in our apartment, I would have to inform the UPDK – a formal request had to be issued asking them to arrange pest control."

"You couldn't go beyond forty kilometres from your home without permission," said my mother with a shudder. "Many areas were completely off-limits. All embassy personnel were given coupons to buy petrol and even the appointment of a Russian language tutor was arranged by the all-powerful UPDK. It was like having asthma, our chests felt suffocated. We were scared to breathe, sometimes."

For my father, a junior officer, a first assignment to the Soviet Union was politically exhilarating. First as a probationer, then as the Third Secretary, he was at the bottom of the pecking order, with several bosses piled on top of him. He found himself sprinting up steep learning curves. There was so much to learn from his seniors, the whole wide world of diplomacy lay in front of him, a labyrinth he had to lose himself in first, before he could find his way out of it.

Indo-Soviet relations were on an upswing, a honeymoon period, and a good time for Indians to be in Moscow. Indians enjoyed a special relationship with the Soviets, a friendship that coincided with the start of the Cold War, when both superpowers began aggressively wooing former colonies to recruit them into their 'camp'. The Americans chose Pakistan, which they saw as a bulwark against communism, strategic to their defence interests, and began to funnel military and economic aid to it.

Wary of Pakistan, nervous of China, and determined to protect its own interests, India turned to the Soviet Union in its effort to modernise and industrialise, even while the tenet of non-alignment championed by Prime Minister Jawaharlal Nehru remained at the core of its foreign policy. A crushing defeat at the hands of the Chinese in the Sino-Indian war in 1962 further cemented India's tilt towards Russia. A willing and eager Russia soon became India's largest supplier of weapons and technology.

Yet, despite the flowering of ties between India and the Soviet Union, Indian diplomats knew they could not take this relationship for granted. The inscrutable demeanour of the Russians kept everyone in the embassy on edge.

The 1965 India-Pakistan war was a gruelling battle that spanned three weeks and ended with the Indian Army capturing the strategic Haji Pir Pass in Jammu and Kashmir that had been under Pakistani occupation. Wresting control of the Haji Pir Pass, located at an altitude of 2637m in the western Himalayas, was a major military triumph for the Indian Army which just two and a half years earlier had suffered a humiliating loss against Chinese troops. Russia, which had been following the war with keen interest, was broadly supportive of India in the conflict. It suddenly saw this war as a prized opportunity to play umpire. Providing a forum for peace talks would make the Russians look good, and give Premier Kosygin legitimacy on an international platform. With the United States bogged down in the Vietnam War, the Russians took the lead in post-war deliberations, inviting Pakistan President Ayub Khan and India's Prime Minister Lal Bahadur Shastri to Tashkent for negotiations. That was how the political and diplomatic denouement of the war landed at the doorstep of the Indian embassy in Moscow.

With the talks set to begin in just under nine days, the Ambassador was cutting his officers no slack. The embassy became a feverish zone of activity; it was a heart-pumping fortnight for the senior officers, as they fired on all cylinders, working day and night in preparation for Tashkent.

Sharma and my father, both probationers, could only observe the goings-on from a distance. They longed to be part of the historic event, but were busy with mundane jobs reserved for rookie officers. The First Secretary felt sorry for them and assigned them some protocol duties. Sharma and my father were thus able to experience the thrill of playing a tiny role in a big operation.

One brutally cold night, they huddled in their over-heated

office. The wind howled, rattling the large heritage windows of the chancery building. It was close to midnight. Sipping cups of tea, both looked harried and exhausted, aware that the other embassy staff and their boss were not going home anytime soon.

Sharma began flipping through a dossier marked 'Tashkent Logistics', in bold red letters. "Two planeloads of VVIPs flying to Tashkent from India. One's taking PM Shastri, Foreign Minister and Defence Minister. The other one has Army General and Deputy Chief of Army."

"What about Foreign Secretary?" asked my father.

"Arriving Moscow in three days. Better get your best suit out my friend."

Both Sharma and my father knew fully well that their career prospects, where they would be posted to next, were closely linked to the successful conclusion of this visit. There was a tacit understanding that pleasing all the top brass from Delhi, including Big Boss Foreign Secretary and Immediate Boss Ambassador was of utmost urgency; any diplomatic faux pas would mean getting banished to the very back of beyond.

My father leaned back in his chair and looked at the snow quietly mounting on the sidewalk. "I really hope things go smoothly at Tashkent," he said.

Sharma nodded. They both fell silent. "*Yaar*, Ravi, it's such a watershed moment," said Sharma. "We're lucky to be here witnessing history."

Sharma and my father lost track of time as they pored over files till they had memorised every minute of the schedule at Tashkent. The night deepened, enveloping the embassy in a dark embrace. Snow continued to fall steadily.

History would twist a victorious triumph for India into a cruel blow for its leadership. At Tashkent, Prime Minister Shastri conceded to withdraw the Indian forces and return the captured posts of Haji Pir Pass and Tithwa, in return for Pakistan's assurance that it would not resort to the use of force against India in the future. What the Indian Army had feared most unravelled at the negotiating table in the dacha.

The same night after the signing of the peace accord, Prime Minister Shastri held a press conference in which he shared the minutes of the negotiations. The decision to cede Haji Pir and Tithwa stirred up a chorus of displeasure back home, with many accusing the Prime Minister of being too 'soft' on Pakistan. Late that night, India's greatly admired and respected Prime Minister collapsed in his dacha. He reportedly had a massive heart attack even before his personal doctor could reach his room. A man who had shown magnanimity and courage in victory would breathe his last in a foreign country, far from the shores of his beloved India, taking the answers of his final moments with him.

Tashkent became the focus of the world's attention as news of Prime Minister Shastri's sudden death spread like wildfire. The Indian embassy went into shock, with everyone walking around in a daze, stunned by the horrific turn of events. Whether the Prime Minister collapsed of a heart attack or was poisoned, his death is shrouded in mystery and remains one of the least investigated high-profile deaths in recent Indian history.

For Sharma and my father, on their maiden postings, Tashkent was a seminal moment in their understanding of Cold

War geopolitics. They witnessed first-hand the ruthless race for supremacy between superpowers, and that countries, especially poor nations like India, were mere pawns in this tussle. Following Prime Minister Lal Bahadur Shastri's shocking death, India's Congress Party elected Indira Gandhi as the new Prime Minister. Under her leadership, the bonhomie with the Russians would continue for the next three decades.

---

The first three letters of the English alphabet held deep significance to our lives in the Foreign Service, as they determined which country we would head to next. As we hit the two-year mark in Moscow, the uncertainty of 'Where next' hovered on our horizon. Would it be an 'A' posting or 'B'? What if it was 'C'?

"They can't be that nasty to us," my mother would say to my father, "to send us to a 'C' place after Moscow. Ambassador likes us, he knows you've worked so hard, he will surely put in a good word for us at the Ministry. They know we have a small baby." And so it went on, the anxiety, the nervousness, the tossing and the turning. When postings of other colleagues were announced, there would be much anticipation as my parents tried to fit the pieces of the puzzle.

"Shah is leaving Rome soon," said my father. "Mani is hoping to go there. Teheran is also coming up in three months."

"Oh no," my mother said, her face becoming small. "Please not Teheran."

A week later there was a flurry of excitement in the embassy. My father had been summoned to the Ambassador's chamber and was inside for a good long while. Later that afternoon, my father bounded up the steps to our apartment.

"I have some news," he told my mother, feigning calm, as he removed his coat and scarf, frisking off the bits of snow that clung to him.

"Please don't bring the snow in," admonished my mother. Then, noting his expression, she immediately sensed something was up. "What's happened? Has Delhi…"

"Ambassador called me into his office. He congratulated me. Delhi is sending us to Washington!"

"Oh my gosh!" My mother didn't know whether to laugh or cry. She crumpled onto the sofa and scooped me in her arms. "I'm so happy! All your hard work was recognised by MEA. Thank God!"

So now we were headed to the *other side* of the Cold War. A land we had heard was so free, even the air there smelt free.

Even though freedom beckoned, we were sad to say goodbye to Moscow, our very first home. This was where my mother had plunged into foreign waters and learned to swim. She had given birth to me, a permanent reminder of their very first stop on the Foreign Express. They had bequeathed me the one word in my passport – Russia – that would always provoke a raised eyebrow by an immigration officer and curiosity among friends, for the rest of my life.

For my father, Russia was the maiden launch into a career that would span forty years. Now, he was heading to the other superpower where he would represent the interests of his country, and play a part in cementing and building relations between India and the United States.

With me wrapped tightly in my mother's arms, my parents

boarded the plane that would take us to the continent of the free. My mother trembled, both from the cold and the excitement, her slim frame heavy with the prospect of starting all over again, in a brand new land.

We turned to wave to our friends who had gathered to say goodbye, the embassy family that had become such an intimate part of our lives.

We didn't know when we would ever see them again.

*Author with her mother in New York, 1969*

# The Other Side of the Cold War

### USA
### 1967–1970

## Washington, DC

There's my mother, in a spiffy red coat against a shower of cherry blossoms. Next to her is a toddler wearing white tights and a yellow sweater, with curly black hair shining in the winter sun. The two of us were standing in front of our small split-level cottage in suburban Washington, DC.

"Want to go for a drive?" my mother asked me. I nodded vigorously. I was ever ready to go on an outing with my mother.

"Ok, then, let's go to the park."

"Coke," I cried out. My vocabulary was expanding every day with words that mattered most in my two-year-old world. My mother said I used to get *drunk* on Coca Cola. But I think it was just the high from being in a land of the free, where I could sense how happy my young parents were; this joy simply spilled onto me. Like falcons, we had flown across the forbidding Russian continent, over the rugged cliffs of the Atlantic, into the embrace of clear open.

For a two-year-old I talked a lot. My mother would tell me that she forgot sometimes how little I was. "You seemed so mature, like a five- or six-year-old. I wanted to tell you everything because you seemed to understand." I was used to being my mother's sounding board because we spent so much time together. Music filled our home; my mother would listen to all her favourite songs from Hindi films like *Padosan, An Evening in Paris, Guide* and *Mughal-e-Azam* on the spool player we had in our living room.

We got into the second-hand Plymouth my father had bought after arriving in Washington, my mother's tiny frame barely visible behind the steering wheel of the behemoth. Our Plymouth looked majestic, the quintessential American car, a huge ship-like creature with big gold wings. I felt very grand and important in that car. One of the first things my mother did after coming to America was to learn to drive, so eager was she to take those wings and fly. Strapped in my car seat in the back, I couldn't have been happier being her little shadow. She looked at me through the rear-view mirror and smiled. Heady and carefree, my mother wanted to soak in America from head to toe, in case she was whisked off before she got her fill.

My mother was awe-struck by the abundance of America. The bright and beautiful displays in the massive department stores were nothing like she had ever seen before. On their meagre salary, my parents couldn't afford to buy anything in these shops, but that didn't deter my mother, who would stroll me through Sears and Macy's, admiring the plentiness of America, which, after the emptiness of Russia, was seductive. From shortages to excesses, from long queues to no queues, the two-and-a-half years we spent in America were the much-needed spark to the stifling austerity of Moscow. To be in the crucible of democracy after the authoritarianism of Russia was like a rainbow butterfly flitting across a green meadow.

Our favourite pastime was going to Safeway, the supermarket near our house. Its wide glass arch doors emblazoned with the big red 'S' sign would lure us in, and we would wander around its cavernous interior for hours. It turned out to be an educational

*Author in Washington, 1968*

outing because we got to know what Americans shopped and ate, and my mother figured they did a lot of both. "How many different types of milk and cheese they have," she would exclaim as she read out from the board displayed above the dairy section. "Cheddar, American, Swiss, Gruyère. Do Americans really eat all these?"

For me the biggest attraction at Safeway was the candy carousel with its dizzying array of bright pink, peppermint and orange sweets in all shapes and sizes. Mom would buy me one and one for herself and we would giggle when the sweetness of candy flooded our mouths.

---

One evening my father came home in a state of great excitement.

"Alka, guess what, you will not believe this!"

"Don't tell me we are getting posted already," exclaimed my mother, looking worried.

"No, no, thankfully not. Stalin's daughter has defected. She's fled Russia and is seeking asylum in America."

"My goodness! The Russians must be furious."

"They are, indeed," said my father. "Imagine, the daughter of Soviet dictator Joseph Stalin defects to USA. How humiliating for the Russians! Svetlana Alliluyeva is at the American embassy in Delhi asking for political asylum."

"In Delhi? Goodness, what on earth is she doing there?"

"Alka, don't you remember she married that Indian fellow, Brajesh Singh, that communist journalist who worked on Moscow Radio. We even met him at a reception. He was Svetlana's third husband. Apparently Brajesh died recently and the authorities allowed her to travel to India to take care of his final rites. But she's landed up at the US embassy in Delhi! There's commotion at the Ministry, they don't know how to handle this."

"What's going to happen to her?" asked my mother, chopping cauliflower and potatoes into tidy squares for the curry she was preparing for our dinner.

"Well the Ministry doesn't want to keep her in India, they can't afford to upset the Russians. The Ambassador was telling us today that it's likely she'll be sent to a neutral place like Switzerland."

"Quite a gutsy lady, I have to say, to escape," said my mother. "The Russians might go after her, no? She will have to be very careful."

"Yes, apparently she managed to evade the KGB agents in Delhi quite cleverly and landed up at the US embassy before they got a whiff of her activities. The Russians are angry with our Ministry for letting this happen, but it's their intelligence failure, not really *ours*."

As expected, to avoid incurring the wrath of the Soviets, the Indian government did not grant Svetlana Alliluyeva permission to remain in India. There were rumours the KGB was planning to kidnap her, but she escaped to Switzerland, reportedly escorted by American CIA agents, where she spent three months before ultimately landing in New York in April 1968. The high-profile defection of the Soviet leader's daughter to enemy territory was watched with great fascination around the world. Alliluyeva was granted asylum by President Lyndon Johnson on humanitarian grounds, while Soviet leader Alexei Kosygin denounced her a "sick person".

Little did we realise when we landed in America that during our brief posting, we would be spectators to extraordinary developments that would define the twentieth century. Momentous events lay ahead. Once again, the history book was getting chapterised even as we turned the page.

---

The American Dream was slowly taking shape for millions of families as they acquired a home, a car and all the conveniences of modern life. The gold rush to suburbanisation had begun: the neatly manicured suburbs with houses resembling toy homes, with their lawns and driveways, as if someone had sketched them perfectly, without smudging; the silence of the suburbs, where you could hear a leaf fall. Many years later when I went to the US as a graduate student, what I hated most about America was its suburbia; I found it suffocating.

My mother, of course, delighted in the modernity of it all and was thrilled by the state-of-the-art gadgets that were transforming American households; in our home too, we had a telephone, a television, an oven, a vacuum cleaner and a shiny gas range. There was piped gas and we drank water straight from the tap. "How advanced America is," she would marvel.

It wasn't long before my mother cut off her long hair, her thick braid that had been her trademark all these years, and got a crop. She swapped her sari for slacks, wore sunglasses and bought herself a smart red coat and boots. For the first time in her life she saw women wearing bikinis on a hot summer day in the park, and couples kissing. She was fully seduced by America's soft power – the hippies, the bra-burners and the bell-bottoms, Jimi Hendrix, Motown and the Beatles, happy to breathe in the bohemia from a safe distance, not having much to do with it but content to be on the periphery of it all.

Just as they were getting to know a new country, my parents too were discovering each other. Their first two years of marriage had been marked by tumultuous beginnings, the newness of the Foreign Service life and a baby. It had left them with little surplus energy to focus on each other. But in Washington they blossomed, like the azaleas that bloomed in our backyard, becoming newlyweds who wanted to make up for lost time.

---

It was a chilly spring day in April. My mother and I had driven past the Tidal Basin and savoured the cherry blossoms from a distance, a curtain of creamy white and pink. When we returned late in the afternoon, my father was already home. He came running out to the driveway, grabbed me out of the car seat and rushed us into the house.

"Alka, what were you doing roaming around the city! Didn't you hear the news?"

"What's the matter?" asked my mother in consternation.

"Martin Luther King has been assassinated," said my father, turning on the television. "They're expecting riots."

"Oh my God," said my mother, "no wonder the streets had felt so unusually quiet."

For the next four days the city burned as rioters smashed windows and looted stores in one of the worst race riots the nation had experienced. Radio reports said crowds were swelling within two blocks of the White House. The National Guard was deployed to assist the local police as Mayor Walter Washington imposed a curfew on the nation's capital. We stayed huddled indoors as America mourned the passing away of one of the most powerful civil rights leaders of the twentieth century who fought for advancing the rights of his fellow African Americans. His death paved the way for the passage of the landmark Civil Rights Act of 1968, and a few months later, Richard Nixon would win the elections on a platform of civil rights and law and order, which became a central theme in his victory campaigns across America.

Sitting in the epicentre of the other superpower, it became obvious that despite its enormous power and wealth, America, too, like its arch rival Russia, had deep-rooted problems. Freedom came at a price, just as repression did in Russia.

---

My mother's famous *tanpura*, subdued by months of neglect in Moscow, suddenly had pride of place in our living room in Washington. It sprung to life as she settled into her new life. It was nearly as tall as she was and much taller than me. My mother would often tell me that if she hadn't married my father she would have become a 'playback singer', and would have been famous. "I was supposed to go to Bombay for an audition, but your Dad's proposal came along and I had to choose between him and the audition," she smiled.

Every now and then she would take out the *tanpura* and strum it gently, and the sonorous sound would echo around our home. She would practise her favourite ragas. "This is Raag Todi," she would explain to me. I found it rather mournful but it seemed to make my mother happy. No wonder then, that she became very excited when our neighbour Mrs White, a second grade school teacher, invited her to give a talk to her students about Indian music. As we drove to Oaks Elementary, I was given the responsibility of alerting my mother should the *tanpura* roll off the back seat.

There was a great deal of excitement among the children when they saw this lanky instrument, which resembled a giant soup spoon, that emitted rather strange drone sounds. My mother sat down on a small carpet the teacher had placed in front of the classroom and sang the notes, *Sa Re Ga Ma Pa,* which made the children giggle. After the lesson, she even allowed them to strum the *tanpura*, which was a rare privilege granted to a very few. Later, Mrs White told us that some of the parents had enquired if my mother would like to give private lessons to their kids.

That night my mother, already convinced about the nice nature of the Americans, recounted our outing to Oaks Elementary with great enthusiasm to my father. Americans, she declared, were such nice people! So friendly to outsiders! My father, far more reserved in his judgement of people, smiled and nodded, more to indulge his wife than out of conviction. After the Russian reserve, my mother was thrilled at the general congeniality of the Americans.

In her own way, my mother was a mini officer representing her country. She wore her Indian-ness with great pride and was always eager to share information about her country with the Americans, who remained mostly oblivious to the existence of

India. Those who were more politically astute believed India was siding with the Russians in the Cold War and were not too happy when my mother explained that we were non-aligned, and that it really wasn't our fault that the Americans chose *Pakistan* over us.

---

We could very easily have been one of the immigrant Indian families putting down our roots in America, just like the Punjabi family down the road. The Khannas had come to America to pursue their education; they were part of the early waves of Indian immigrants who would make this country their home. Indians were flocking to America in growing numbers, the best and the brightest, the beginning of the brain drain that would continue for decades to come. Some of them became my parents' close friends and would drop in to discuss their PhD dissertations, their past in India and future in America. My mother was envious of them. "They get to live in America, whereas we will have to leave," she would often say.

Our American neighbour Jim once saw my father struggling with a lawn mower. "Need a hand with that, Sir?" he called out. Relieved, my father nodded. By the time Jim had shown my father how to operate the mower, they had become good friends and were drinking beer like college buddies. Jim's initial suspicion about us having lived in Moscow eased once he realised my father was a diplomat, not a spy. Then he was agog with questions about the Soviet Union, which he referred to as that 'barbaric' country infested with 'communist madmen'.

---

When we arrived in Washington, America was at the peak of its involvement in Vietnam, with thousands of American soldiers fighting the proxy war in Southeast Asia. Anti-war sentiment was raging, with demonstrations spilling across campuses in America, a startling contrast to Russia, where my parents had never seen any form of dissent. Observing Russia from the Free World provided a starkly different perspective on the Cold War. Suspicion lurked high vis-a-vis the Soviets. Sitting in America, it was easy to loathe the communists, to feed into the hysteria about the commies.

"It was a bit strange analysing geopolitical events while sitting in Washington," my father recalled. "Sometimes I found myself defending the Russians, simply because I knew what their position would be on specific issues."

By the late sixties, US hegemony and global influence was spreading, making it the de facto democratic powerhouse of the world. My father went to work firing on all cylinders. Having just come from Moscow, he was given more attention than he normally would have enjoyed as Second Secretary. His insights on sensitive Indo-Soviet matters were found useful to the senior officers, who summoned him occasionally to their offices to brainstorm.

"Ravi, Soviet Union *mein kya ho raha hai*? What are these Russians thinking?" they would ask. "They are going back to the days of the Second World War," my father replied. "Invading Eastern Europe is a disaster."

Thus, a year into our posting, on August 20, 1968, when the Soviet Union led Warsaw Pact troops into Czechoslovakia to crush the democracy movement that was taking root there, my father was able to brief his seniors about the invasion with an incisiveness that could only come from someone who had spent time on the ground understanding Russian realpolitik.

---

The chancery building of the embassy, purchased by the Indian government in 1946, was striking for its French architectural style and comprised two adjacent buildings located on Massachusetts Avenue. A fleet of velvet stairs led to the main foyer and into the interiors, which were always humming with activity. It was a very extensive and busy embassy, headed by the Ambassador, a seasoned diplomat personally picked for the post by Indian Prime Minister Indira Gandhi. There were several wings or departments: Commerce, Political, Economic, Education, Science and Technology, Community Affairs and Consular. Like in Moscow, the Defence Department was large, represented by Air, Naval and Military Attaches and their junior officers. There was also a Press, Information and Culture wing where my father worked, a department that liaised with the media, and which was becoming very powerful in America.

Relations between India and the US remained frosty, with the Americans largely dismissive of India, which they saw as poor and backward and a Russian stooge. The biggest irritant for India remained the US preferential treatment towards Pakistan. Sophisticated American ammunition that Pakistan had directed against India in the war just a few years ago was like an open wound that festered. America's stance on Kashmir further wedged the two apart. In debates at the UN Security Council, America's insistence that the Kashmir issue needed a political settlement and its refusal to recognise Kashmir as part of India riled the Indians.

When it came to its other enemy, China, India was equally distressed to see the Americans warming up towards its rival. The Indian embassy had been observing that the pro-China lobby in the US was becoming more influential. This did not bode well for India, which was still licking its wounds from the disastrous loss in the Sino-India war. Even six years on, the defeat remained a big black cloud over India's foreign policy and morale. Indian bureaucrats would often grumble that the Americans misunderstood India's policy of non-alignment.

Meanwhile, India continued its vociferous opposition to the Vietnam War, which the Americans saw as further evidence of India's proclivity towards the Soviets. Against this backdrop, Indian diplomats were wary of their American counterparts. India's stock remained generally low both at the State Department and on Capitol Hill. As a result, the Indian embassy had to double up on diplomacy to keep the relationship on an even keel, and prevent it from dropping to new lows.

---

The official reception was in full swing. The Ambassador's residence, bedecked with flowers and candles offered the perfect ambience for the annual Republic Day soiree. My father walked around the expansive living room, mingling with his counterparts from other embassies, while my mother joined the First Secretary's wife to ensure the guests were being looked after. The Ambassador's wife, dressed elegantly in a cream silk sari was at her hospitable best, the seasoned diplomat's wife. My mother couldn't help but stare at her, secretly hoping some day she would acquire the same poise and élan the First Lady of

India House epitomised. My mother was wearing a sari herself, because embassy personnel were required to wear the national dress on official functions.

Underscoring the artifice and banter, the excitement in the air was palpable. A few months from now the Americans and Russians were going to meet in Moscow to sign the Nuclear Non-Proliferation Treaty (NPT). The landmark summit between President Lyndon Johnson and Soviet leader Leonid Brezhnev loomed ahead, a much-needed beacon of hope in the Cold War. Several countries were expected to come on board to sign the NPT. Except, India. That an impoverished Third World country should have the audacity to stand up to the superpowers was exasperating the Americans.

Superficially, none of this tension was obvious at the Republic Day reception.

The First Secretary from the Embassy of Mexico, a good friend of my father's, was thoroughly enjoying the starters. "Delicious food as always," he said, tucking into a kebab. Lowering his voice, "The State Department is not lobbying you hard enough on the NPT, eh?"

"I believe they are trying very hard," my father said.

"Well, as you know, we've succumbed," said the Mexican officer, somewhat sheepishly.

"Yes, I'm aware," said my father. "Rather a shame."

The Indian Ambassador was standing with Pete Wrangley, a senior defence department official.

"Mr Ambassador, you should come on board the NPT," said Wrangley. "What you are doing, perhaps, may not be prudent and not in the best interest of the global order."

The Ambassador looked Wrangley straight in the eye. "Global

order? What global order are we talking about Mr Wrangley? Perhaps you would like to define what you mean by that. From where we stand, your definition of a global order is one that suits your interests, not ours."

"Come on, Mr Ambassador, it is in everyone's interest to control the spread of nuclear weapons."

"Indeed one cannot argue with that, Mr Wrangley," said the Ambassador. "But as you are aware, we have unique geopolitical considerations which dictate our foreign policy. Given our recent legacy of conflict, we expected a greater level of understanding from the Americans, which has not been forthcoming. We are rather disappointed." He summoned the waiter. "Would you like another chicken *tikka*, Mr Wrangley? I do recall you enjoyed it the last time you visited India House."

For weeks, my father would deconstruct the NPT with my mother, who had started discussing politics with my father with great ardour. She too was becoming intoxicated by the world of international relations.

"Alka, the Americans will never understand what it's like having enemies like Pakistan and China on both sides. The treaty is so discriminating!"

"What would happen if we sign it?" asked my mother.

"Well, it means we'll have the Americans and other nuclear powers dictating to us what we can and cannot do," said my father. "It may put restrictions on us, which means we won't be able to use nuclear energy for development. The Americans are not even willing to give us any nuclear guarantees, so why should we sign?"

A few weeks later, amid much global fanfare, on July 1, 1968, the Americans and the Russians signed the Nuclear Non-Proliferation Treaty in Moscow to control the spread of nuclear weapons and technology, with 62 nations on board. India and Pakistan did not sign the treaty. Barely had the signatories returned to their respective countries when, a month later, the Russians and four other Warsaw Pact nations invaded Czechoslovakia in a blatant show of force, crushing any goodwill that might have been generated from the NPT summit in Moscow. The US immediately condemned Russia's invasion and backed a UN Security Council resolution calling for an immediate withdrawal of the Warsaw Pact forces. But Soviet leader Leonid Brezhnev refused to budge, invoking the Brezhnev Doctrine instead, to justify Russia's use of force in Prague and, eleven years later, the Soviet invasion of Afghanistan. The 'Prague Spring' as it was called, was a blow to any plans of détente between the US and Russia. It became clear that Brezhnev did not plan to loosen his grip over the East Bloc at any cost, even if it meant delaying détente with the West.

The Cold War was showing no signs of letting up.

---

History was swirling around with such intensity, it was difficult to keep pace with the developments. On the extraordinary afternoon of July 20, 1969, we were moonstruck, as we sat with our neighbours Anne and Jim, in their suburban home in Silver Spring, waiting for that century-defining moment to unfold on the television screen. I was sitting on my father's lap. I knew I had to be quiet. The previous night my father had pointed out the moon to me. "Tomorrow a human being will be walking on *that* surface," he told me in a voice full of awe and amazement. "We are all going to be part of history!"

Anne and Jim had arranged for plenty of food. They grilled burgers and hotdogs in their backyard and a festive atmosphere prevailed in the neighbourhood with many homes displaying the Stars and Stripes and banners and balloons. Underneath the celebratory mood everyone was aware that NASA's first-ever manned moon landing was fraught with danger. The astronauts had left Earth on Wednesday and it had taken them four days to reach the moon. Would they be able to pull off such a daring mission was the question on the minds of millions around the world watching the event live on television with baited breath.

Suddenly the screen flickered and everyone fell silent. Then, as we held our breaths, we saw astronaut Neil Armstrong emerge through the grainy black and white satellite imagery. The eagle had landed! On our tiny screen we saw Armstrong descend the ladder of Apollo 11 and take the most enormous step mankind had ever taken. We felt massive goosebumps as he, along with Buzz Aldrin, looking like robots, walked around in the Sea of Tranquility in their spacesuits. They spent nearly two hours collecting samples from a surface Armstrong described as "powdered charcoal". Next, the American duo planted the Stars and Stripes flag on the bumpy, stony surface of that orb which I would look at in wonderment, growing up. All the adults in the room had tears in their eyes. Then they burst into applause and everyone hugged and embraced one another. It was a moment that transcended divisions and differences, and united humanity as one whole. Even Moscow Radio mentioned this spectacular feat on its radio broadcast. Neil Armstrong made the world proud of America. Both on land and in space, America was appearing invincible.

It was my mother's dream to visit New York City. Exactly eighteen years ago, in 1950, her father had won a Fulbright scholarship to study at Columbia University. He traversed the seas from India to America to pursue his PhD in Political Science, along with his young wife Saroj. My mother often spoke to me about her parents, especially her lovely mother Saroj. "My mother was very beautiful," she would tell me. "She looked like Nutan, my favourite movie actress." Saroj died soon after returning to India, when she was just twenty-seven years old.

I knew my mother was sad whenever she spoke about Saroj. I was not used to her being melancholic, so to cheer her up I broke into a song I'd heard her hum all the time these days. "*Aasman ke neeche, hum aaj apne peeche, pyar ka jahan basa ke chale!*" My mother looked at me in amazement. "You sang that so well! My goodness, I think you have inherited singing from me. When Daddy comes home tonight, we'll surprise him with your song!" My strategy of distraction had worked perfectly.

To fulfil my mother's dream, the three of us drove to the Big Apple. My parents could not get enough of the city, and my father wanted to preserve every second of it on his camera. As a result, there are several pictures of me strutting poses in front of all the iconic New York City landmarks. My mother, in her big oval sunglasses, tights and top, looked very glamorous for an admiring husband who captured her many moods from behind his lens. We peered out at New York Harbour through Lady Liberty's crown, while my father told us about America's great legacy of immigration. "Ellis Island is where all the immigrants landed, to make their new life in this country," he said.

We could almost touch the freedom as it wafted around us. The skyline and the sea receded in the horizon, as the boats took over. With its adrenaline rush of skyscrapers, New York City makes you believe in human ability. It makes you believe in the power of the unstoppable. My young parents, heady with youth and enthusiasm, stood there for a long time, hands tightly clutched, gazing out to the sea, oblivious to my impatient tugging at my mother's coat.

At that moment, we didn't know that our lives would soon become topsy-turvy. But for now, there was the bliss of young love that nothing could crush.

---

A few months later, on a summer afternoon, as my mother was driving through Bethesda with me in the back seat, she almost ran a light. She had seemed distracted, and she slowed down, realising what she had just been about to do.

"We are going to Sikkim, a place very far from here." She looked in the rear-view mirror at me. I stopped singing the new nursery rhyme I had learned. I could sense she was anxious. I looked at her, trying to absorb what she was telling me. Today, my mother seemed so different, not her usual bubbly self.

"How will you adjust there, in such a backward place! I wish we never had to leave." My mother slowed down as we entered the driveway to our small cottage which had been our home for two-and-a-half years. My father had just received a posting order from New Delhi that morning, informing him that his term in Washington was up and he was being transferred to a country called Sikkim, a small independent kingdom in the Himalayas.

"We have to first go to Calcutta, then by train to Siliguri, and drive up to the capital Gangtok," my mother continued talking, me pretending to understand every single word.

When my father came home from the office that evening, he too seemed preoccupied. He didn't play with me or sing as he always did. Instead, he looked worried as he and my mother spoke to each other in serious voices.

"This is horrible news!" my mother was close to tears. "Will Sikkim be worse than Moscow?" she asked in a scared voice.

"Yes, I think so," said my father gloomily. He looked at me, playing with my big doll. Sikkim was an impoverished country northeast of India. Much later it would become a part of India, but at that time, it was a monarchy where medical facilities and living conditions were primitive. He didn't dare tell my mother that Sikkim was so underdeveloped that the government hadn't been able to find anyone to fill the post he had been selected for. It had been lying vacant for the last few months. Sikkim was truly and fully a hardship 'C' posting.

"How can they do this to us?" said my mother. "Can't you please speak to Delhi? Ask them for an extension? We can't go to a place like Sikkim, we have a small child," she pleaded. "And another on the way." To leave the cushy comfort of America seemed like punishment to my mother, who could only think of one thing, the well-being of her children: mine and that of her second child, due later that year.

My father recalled his meeting a month ago with the Indian Foreign Secretary during a high-profile visit to Washington. He had said to my father: "Young man, I'm going to send you to a place where your Hindi and Sanskrit will come in very useful."

Reading his thoughts, my mother said, "Remember what FS told you?"

My father nodded, "I never guessed it would be Sikkim."

"So mean of him," said my mother bitterly. "You should've never met FS when he came to Washington. You became his scapegoat."

My father didn't say anything, his mind shooting off on tangents. He knew his wife was right, but he also believed he had been selected for the job because of the work he had done in Washington. Sikkim was, ironically, a form of recognition, even though my mother would never see it that way. He thought back to his meeting with the Ambassador who had summoned him to his chamber and gently broken the news of the posting. The Ambassador, who had grown very fond of my father, felt a sense of responsibility towards this soft-spoken young officer. Ravi's quiet demeanour and diligence had impressed him and he had shared his opinions with the Foreign Secretary, who had instantly assessed that my father was the right choice for the role in Sikkim.

Sikkim, while it was a protectorate of India since 1950, was a monarchy. Flanked by the two juggernauts China and India, the tiny kingdom, nestled in the Himalayas, was becoming a tinderbox, with Prime Minister Indira Gandhi herself keeping an eagle eye on developments there. Delhi urgently needed to put a team in place in Gangtok that comprised the most trustworthy officers, capable of giving Indian authorities a heads-up on the events that were proceeding at breakneck speed in a country that had become of paramount importance to India's security. India was responsible for the kingdom's defence, communications and external relations, and the Political Office, the equivalent of an Indian embassy, where my father would be going as Second Secretary, would be the most powerful player in determining the political future of this country. Sikkim was, unequivocally, a highly sensitive political post.

"Your being in Gangtok at this vital juncture is important for our country's interests," said the Ambassador. Looking the young officer sitting nervously across from him squarely in the eye, he said kindly, "I'm sure you will do well, I wish you good luck."

Our posting to Sikkim was fait accompli.

There was a collective shock in the embassy when news of our posting to Sikkim broke, many officers quietly exhaling relief that they had not been the 'chosen ones'. Both the Ambassador and the Ministry in Delhi advised my father that my mother and I should live in India while he worked in Gangtok, especially since my mother was going to have a baby. He could visit every few months. It was not a posting they recommended for families with small children. But my mother was adamant. She declared she would accompany her husband no matter where, whether it was to Sikkim or the North Pole. And that was that.

It took us some time to identify Sikkim on the map, but explaining its existence to Americans and even to some of our Indian friends proved a struggle. Our sprightly neighbour Jim surprised us when he told my mother he had heard about this country called Sikkim after reading a fascinating story about Hope Cooke in *The New York Times*. Hope Cooke was an American debutante from Manhattan who had married the Prince of Sikkim a few years ago, and their glamorous wedding had received a fair bit of coverage in the US media.

My mother knew the good times were over. But her sunny-side up spirit resurfaced. "It will be an adventure," she would tell me, as she scurried about the house clearing up cabinets and drawers.

We were packed and ready. A small crowd of friends and embassy officers came to see us off at the airport, some trying unsuccessfully to conceal their sympathy.

Once again, we were off, this time with the Beatles' blockbuster single '*Get Back*' ringing loudly in our ears.

*Author receiving her prize from the Chogyal (the King of Sikkim), 1973*

*Kingdom of Hope*

**SIKKIM**
*1970–1974*

## Gangtok

Suffused by the warm fragrance of silver fern and birch, Dorji and I made our way out of the thicket of trees, our pockets bulging with pointy wooden cones we had painstakingly collected in the forest. A few feet away from us, a carpet of rhododendrons fell across the Himalayan hillside towards the valley below. From our six-thousand-foot vantage point, we could see flashes of the river Teesta in the far distance, a silver ribbon curling through the rugged terrain of Sikkim, a small kingdom tucked between Bhutan and Tibet. I looked longingly at the flowers, contemplating whether to pluck some to take home. But my pockets were full and I needed my hands to be free to climb up the hill, steep in parts, to get home. Suddenly it struck me this patch of fiery red rhododendrons did *not* look familiar.

"Where are we, Dorji?" We both looked around at our sylvan surroundings, which only a few hours ago had seemed so welcoming, but now were beginning to feel sinister. Just then I felt something moist on my left leg and noticed a trickle of blood staining my calf. Distressed, I shook my leg violently. Watching the leeches clamber over my thin shoes made me queasy, even though I was used to them in this wild Himalayan countryside that was my playground.

"Dorji, we must go," I started running, clutching the cones in my pockets, Dorji trailing behind me. Towering in the far distance like a skyscraper was the majestic Kanchendzonga, which the Sikkimese worshipped as their guardian spirit. But at that moment, as its peaks illuminated a dusky sky, they were a forbidding reminder that it was getting late and I needed to be home. I scrambled up a steep slope as fast as my legs could carry me, panting, "Dorji, hurry up, hurry up!" Dorji struggled behind me, afraid he would lose me if he didn't keep up. He knew going to my 'big house' guaranteed him a meal, and he had been hungry for hours.

Even though we were both six years old, I had a maturity beyond my years and felt a strong sense of ownership over Dorji, a local Nepalese boy who was my closest friend. My mother would call him "*shemda* Dorji" because his nose was always runny. No one really knew who his parents were, although my mother believed he was the child of the shopkeeper who sold *momos* down the street. Dorji always appeared out of nowhere, just as I returned from school, and we would spend our afternoons exploring the thick forest behind our house.

It was Dorji who taught me the flora and fauna of the hillside; where to pluck the juiciest gooseberries, look for hidden streams beneath rocks, identify the footprints of a fox and sight the shy Red Panda, a native of Sikkim. Once we spotted one sitting high up on a tree, its russet colour a striking contrast to the frondescence around it. It had a small white face and sharp, pointed ears. I was very impressed by its long bushy tail, which Dorji explained it used to wrap itself around with to stay warm. I thought it was a rather clever thing to do. Unafraid, it gazed down at us from its lofty abode for quite some time before it clambered up further into the tree and disappeared. Dorji also taught me to distinguish the call of a fox from a jackal. I was once frightened by the sound of high-pitched screams, like a baby screaming, which Dorji explained was that of a jackal. My mother said thanks to Dorji I had become a wild child.

"Dorji, I can't see the palace," I peered at the horizon, fear rising in my throat, fervently wishing we had not ventured down a different path today. The palace was our lodestar, a reassurance in this wilderness that home would be just around the next bend in our winding path. Dorji, who had been focused on trying to get through a thorny bush unscathed, stopped and looked around. He too appeared disoriented. "I want to go home!" I started to cry.

Evenings came quickly on the mountainside and the air felt chilly. Suddenly Dorji pointed ahead. "This way!" We communicated in Nepali, the lingua franca in Sikkim. Imbued with a quiet proficiency that came from his intimate knowledge of the mountains, Dorji was able to get us back on track and soon we reached the back of the house wedged halfway up the hill, an old, crumbling cottage, threatening to collapse from the weight of its age. Flooded with relief, I ran through the backyard and into the kitchen and plopped on to the table, exhausted from our excursion. After a thorough scolding, my mother rewarded us with piping hot *momos* and warm milk; Dorji ate quickly, with full concentration, and ran off, presumably back to his own family.

When my parents, baby brother and I arrived in Gangtok, the capital of Sikkim, via Siliguri in the summer of 1970, it was a country so remote and backward that even the best shock absorbers could not have protected us from the jarring contrast to our charmed life in Washington. Or even India, where my mother and I had stayed with my grandmother for six months before my baby brother's birth. In Gangtok, the weather was more predictable than water and electricity; medical facilities were primitive and disease rampant. After the modernity of America, Sikkim was a cruel blow, especially for my mother. Her bright modern kitchen in Washington, full of state-of-the-art gadgets, seemed like a chimera. All our meals had to be cooked on a stove for which our caretaker Tulsi would hunt for charcoal and wood every day. On days it rained, he struggled to light the stove. Tulsi very quickly became an adopted member of our household, doubling up as driver, gardener and babysitter all rolled into one. There was nothing Tulsi couldn't do and my parents relied on him heavily as we struggled from one day to the next.

I have a strong memory of always being cold. The insulation was so poor that cold air would constantly rush in through the walls and windows of our home. During the long spells when electricity was cut off, we would shiver while waiting for the lights to come back on so we could use the small heaters in our bedrooms, even though they were miserably inadequate.

It was a visceral test of fortitude for my mother, having to take care of two small children – one who was just a month old – in a place flagged as a hardship posting, which became our home for four years. She would often say, "a posting to Sikkim is the Ministry's way of putting you in your place."

In Gangtok, we became suspended in time. I didn't understand then that we were sitting on the cusp of history that would forever alter the destiny of both – this Himalayan kingdom, as well as ours.

---

Within a few weeks of our arrival in Gangtok, tragedy struck. One brutally cold winter night, despite all the heaters cranked up in the rooms, the chill seemed to penetrate our very bones. I recall long bouts of shivering, huddled under my blankets, which felt desperately thin.

"Madam, I have not been able to find enough wood or charcoal to light the stove," said Tulsi to my mother. "Everything is wet after the rains." At twenty-eight, Tulsi looked haggard, with deep lines that creased his forehead when he spoke; hard work and poverty had left their mark on him.

My mother looked alarmed. Keeping the baby warm was of utmost importance. "Just make sure we save all the wood for the fireplace in my room," she told Tulsi. I followed my mother into her room where my baby brother was sleeping. I peered over the pram and touched his cheek. Mama had a local girl Renu who helped take care of baby. "He is crying a lot," Renu told my mother. "I think he is feeling cold, Madam." Looking anxious, my mother went back to look for Tulsi to ask him to hurry and find more wood. The temperature continued to drop through the night. The wind howled and the house rattled. My father returned home late that night, long after I had fallen asleep.

I woke up in the middle of the night to the sound of my little brother crying. I don't know when he stopped because I fell asleep again. I heard my mother say to my father that maybe she should have heeded those who had advised her to stay in India with the baby and me, till he was older. Not too many couples brought their infants to Sikkim. The next morning I ran into my parent's room and peered over the crib at my little brother who stopped crying immediately when he saw me. He stared at me with his black button eyes that reminded me of the little rabbit in our backyard, which Tulsi had brought home one day.

"Why is he crying, Mama?"

"Doctor says he has a cold," my mother said and sighed. "I wish this winter would hurry and go away." But it was just the beginning of a long cold spell; my mother knew that, as she looked down anxiously at the infant, whimpering slightly, fussy and tired from crying. She picked him up in her arms and hugged him close.

My mother urged my father to do something about the cold house. "We need some additional heaters, we need to put one near baby's crib; it's freezing in our room." As my parents tended to my baby brother that night, I crept back into bed and fell asleep, listening to my parents speaking in low voices, so as not to disturb baby who had slept off, exhausted from crying. An unsettling quiet enveloped our home.

That night my baby brother suddenly developed a high fever followed by severe diarrhoea that convulsed him through the night. My parents called the doctor who advised them to rush to the hospital immediately. By the time my frantic parents reached the hospital in the early hours of the morning, baby had succumbed to an infection none of the doctors were able to identify. My little brother's death struck a catastrophic blow to our family. I have a strong memory of hugging my mother to ease her fits of sobbing. My father plunged into deep despair, unable to concentrate on his new job or his shattered wife. He went about his daily routine, a ghost of a man, shrinking from the weight of the colossal tragedy, losing twenty pounds over the next few weeks. His boss, the Political Officer, and his helpful, affectionate wife sensed Ravi's profound sorrow as they saw him pacing up and down for hours, not touching any food, unable to focus on those in front of him. They reached out to him and my mother, drawing them close with their affection, laying the foundation of a friendship that would blossom and survive the next fifty years.

My mother slowly pulled herself together. She allowed the sweet peas in the garden to ease her pain, the Kanchendzonga to bless her through the kitchen window, the rabbits in our backyard to nuzzle her fingers and Dorji and me to sing her Nepali nursery rhymes. She was the cure my father needed, the balm for his deep wound. They learned to hold hands and smile again. When my sister was born two years later, they named her Aparna, the daughter of the Himalayas.

I was no longer alone.

---

My world revolved around our house on the hill. It was sweet and secure.

At the bottom of the hill, a small brook ran past, and we would sleep to its gurgling sounds. Every morning, I would hop-scotch across the pebbles in the stream and trek up a hundred steps (I counted them every day) that led to my school, Tashi Namgyal Academy, which had been founded by the former King (the Choygal's father) in 1926 and remained a proud reminder of his legacy.

Halfway up was my favourite resting spot, a small clearing from where I could see the palace in the distance, its regal perch above the town lending it an aloof grandeur. The palace had a simplicity and elegance that defined much of Sikkimese architecture. The sacred peaks of the Kanchendzonga, so beloved to the Sikkimese, rose protectively behind the palace, so close you felt you could reach out and touch them.

Palden Thondup Namgyal, popularly known as the Chogyal, the Tibetan word for a religious king, was the young Prince who took over the reins of governing his country following his revered father's death. I vividly recalled the Chogyal's face, with eyes that crinkled kindly when he smiled. Just a week before, the Chogyal had visited our school for the annual prize-giving ceremony. Along with the other children, I practised perfecting the art of bowing with a flourish and was thrilled when the King personally presented us our certificates for completing grade two. There is a photo of me on stage in my school uniform, in my smart blazer, grey skirt and black shoes, and my hair in two thick plaits, in a deep bow, with the King smiling and bowing back in return.

Dorji would tell me colourful stories about the palace and how he had seen the royal children playing in the lawns wearing shining jewels and robes, with servants carrying trays full of sweets. Dorji had a fanciful imagination and would bask in my wide-eyed attention. The children had blue eyes and fair skin, he would tell me, and sometimes rode on elephants. Once he had even seen them flying on a carpet around the palace lawns. The bit about the flying carpet came from one of my favourite storybooks, which I would often read to Dorji. I held on to every word Dorji said, and both of us would drift into faraway lands of castles full of gold coins, rainbow lamps and bejewelled princes and princesses.

---

The Chogyal's fairy tale wedding to American Hope Cooke captured world attention and thrust Sikkim into the spotlight. The royal couple's glamorous wedding in a monastery amid Lamas and maharajas was celebrated with much fanfare over several days in Gangtok. Hope Cooke, a student at Sarah Lawrence College, came from a wealthy family in New York. One summer, she decided to head off to India to study Eastern philosophy and culture, and found herself at the Windamere Hotel in Darjeeling. It was there, while she was sitting in the hotel lobby, that the Chogyal would walk in and instantly fall in love with her. Their starry romance continued even after she returned to America to complete her studies. Two years later they got married and Hope Cooke became the Queen of Sikkim.

Hope Cooke was an enigma, a delicate waif-like princess who was enchanted by her new home in the Himalayas, but would quickly grow disillusioned as her husband began to sink deeper into the quagmire of local politics.

Like all the Sikkimese, I was infatuated with the Queen, whom the locals called the Gyalmo. How I longed for a glimpse of her! I got the opportunity when my mother agreed to take me to the annual Lama dance, a much-coveted event hosted by the Chogyal and the Gyalmo. I felt giddy with happiness as our jeep lurched uphill towards the palace.

The afternoon felt like a picnic on the hill, with much merriment and laughter as food and *tungba*, the local brew, flowed. Monks chanting in tandem with the roar of drums and trumpets marked the auspicious start of the ceremony, as dancers in brightly painted masks swayed to the rhythms to appease the mountain spirits. Swinging their ceremonial swords, they leapt and bounded about, frightening at times, gentle and graceful at others. I clutched my mother's sari when they came too close. Beautiful Sikkimese women swirled about in gold and purple *bakus* as the afternoon stretched into the evening and dusk touched the hillside.

The Gyalmo mingled with her guests – diplomats, journalists, local politicians – the epitome of grace in her exquisite moss green velvet *baku* and mustard silk blouse, her hair pinned back in an elegant bun. My mother made a request to one of the palace officials if we could meet the Gyalmo for just a few minutes. As we made our way to the front of the tent where Queen Hope was sitting by herself, enjoying a brief respite from the rigours of protocol, I was overcome by shyness.

*The Chogyal, Palden Thondup Namgyal and the Gyalmo, Hope Cooke, 1971*

"Your Highness, there's a young lady who would like to meet you," the official said to the Queen and ushered us towards her.

The Gyalmo looked at me and smiled. "Oh hello! How very nice to meet you," she said in her soft whispering voice, which was her trademark manner of speaking. I buried my face in my mother's sari and refused to look up. The Queen laughed and said gently, "I love the dress you are wearing." Feeling my mother's impatient nudge, I slowly looked up at the Gyalmo. Her smile reminded me of cherries, while her sky-blue eyes and rosy cheeks made me think of my favourite doll that I had carried with me all the way from America.

The serenity of the mountains embracing the palace and the valleys below masked the massive ferment that was slowly building, one that would eventually shatter the fragility of the Kingdom. For now, the Chogyal and Gyalmo maintained equanimity while hosting their guests, personally ensuring that everyone was well looked after. These were halcyon days in this small but fiercely proud country. But the clouds were becoming heavier with each passing day. The cloudburst was imminent.

---

Something had disturbed her sleep. My mother looked at her watch and noted it was close to midnight. Then she heard the noise, growing louder, a strange ghoulish fusion of drums and shouts. It seemed to be coming from the garden outside the house. She wondered if it were the Lamas, the Buddhist priests, but they rarely came out at night. Besides, the noise sounded very different from the soothing chants of the Lamas.

There was a knock on the bedroom door. It was Tulsi. He was shouting, "*Saab, Saab*!" (Sir, Sir).

My mother heard it as *saap* (snake) and shook her husband awake, "Snake, snake!"

My father jumped out of bed, hurriedly wore his night-robe and said to my mother. "I'll go see what's happening."

He opened the door. Tulsi stood outside, holding a candle in his hand. "*Saab, Saab*!" Tulsi appeared breathless, unable to utter anything apart from 'Sir'.

"What's the matter, Tulsi?" asked my father, realising it was not a snake that had distressed his household help.

"*Saab*, the Queen..." said Tulsi, finally.

"What about the Queen?" asked my father, looking irritated. Tulsi must have had a bad dream; these locals were obsessed with the King and Queen.

"*Saab*, she is standing at the door."

"What nonsense, Tulsi!" scolded my father.

"Really, *Saab*."

My father strode past Tulsi into the living room. To his complete horror, the Gyalmo stood in front of him, with a group of Sikkimese men and women behind her, all dressed in strange ghostly costumes. She was wearing a black cape and a pointy witch hat, with black gloves and boots and she held a drum in her hand. Nothing like the golden silk *bakus* and pearls she usually wore. The American wife of the King of Sikkim, Hope Cooke, in his living room! My father rubbed his eyes, wondering if all this was a dream.

"Your Highness, what, er, what brings you here at this time..." Before my father could finish his sentence, the Gyalmo had grabbed him by the shoulder, "Let's have some fun!" she said, twirling my bewildered father around the living room, as the beat of the drums drowned out any further conversation. My mother, who had just walked into the living room, was horrified to see the Gyalmo and her husband circling around the room. Tulsi hovered by the fireplace looking dumbstruck. The drums continued to roar, and suddenly, Gyalmo thrust my father's hand into my mother's, asking them to continue dancing. As quickly as she had appeared in their living room, Gyalmo and her troupe vanished into the blackness of the night.

Later, it came to light that it was Halloween night in her home country, which had got the American Queen into a mood to celebrate her native festival. It was also the last time my parents would see the Queen laughing and enjoying herself as freely as she did in our living room. The tumultuous political events that were to follow would transform her life dramatically.

"The First Secretary of the Political Office dancing to the tune of the Queen of Sikkim" became a 'royal' piece of gossip about my father in Gangtok.

Strategically located, our house straddled two important roads. One led to India House, the residence of the Political Officer, formerly the Gangtok Residency that the British had established in the 1890s during their colonial rule. The British had appointed a Political Officer to administer Sikkim, a country with a key location from which they could man four posts: Lhasa and three other towns in Tibet.

The other bigger road went to Nathu La, the Sikkim-Tibet border just seventy kilometres from Gangtok. A large number of Indian troops were stationed there; every day, we could hear the military trucks trundling up the steep slope as they wound their way towards Nathu La. Indian Army officers riding in their jeeps was a common sight because, by the late sixties, India's armed presence was fully entrenched across Sikkim.

Despite the difficult terrain and conditions, the army officers, many of whom were stationed without their families, had an irrepressible *joie de vivre* and a cheerful disposition, which allowed them to overcome the pangs that came from prolonged absences from their loved ones. Since there wasn't much else to do in Gangtok, and there were no restaurants or shops, they would throw parties, the laughter and merriment drawing everyone together in a tight fraternity. My parents mingled freely with the army officers and many would become their closest friends. Socialising became the mantra to surviving Sikkim, with affairs and romances blooming against the backdrop of intense political drama. The other favoured pastime was watching Hindi films. Movies like *Hare Rama Hare Krishna*, and *Aradhana*, had acquired a cult status, wreaking havoc on morality and social values.

The screen flickered and the crowd screamed as Bollywood superstar Rajesh Khanna began singing *Mere Sapno Ki Rani* to his lady love, Sharmila Tagore, who stared at him coyly from the compartment of her train, as it whistled along through the picturesque hills of Darjeeling. *Aradhana* fever was sweeping across Sikkim, the hit songs echoing through the mountains and plains. Everywhere, people were humming the tunes with great gusto and swooning over its star pair. That the lead song *Mere Sapno Ki Rani* was filmed in nearby Darjeeling gave everyone in Gangtok a great sense of ownership and proximity. My parents, like thousands of young couples, found it easy to slip into the shoes of Rajesh and Sharmila – the blush of youth wrapping them tightly. My father would tease my mother that she reminded him of Sharmila because of her deep dimples and classical nose. The infectious *Kora Kagaz Tha* and *Roop Tera Mastana* songs pulsated around our home, infusing a joyful atmosphere, even as the political climate started to churn outside.

---

Sikkim had the geographic misfortune of having China and India as its contiguous neighbours. Both juggernauts had their imperial sights set firmly on the kingdom. The leadership of newly independent India, under Prime Minister Jawaharlal Nehru, recognised the geostrategic importance of Sikkim as a buffer to China. The communists, under Mao Tse Tung, had taken control of China and the 'Red Scare' was intensifying. Chinese troops were moving towards Tibet. For India, there was simply no time to lose. In 1950, Nehru convinced the Maharaja of Sikkim to sign the Indo-Sikkim Treaty under which India became responsible for Sikkim's defence, communications and external relations. Under the agreement, an Indian civil servant was stationed in Gangtok, occupying the position held earlier by the British administrative official. Referred to as Political Officer, the Indian bureaucrat became the top man in Sikkim. The treaty stipulated that Sikkim's internal affairs would remain under the purview of the monarchy, while at the same time India would have the overall responsibility to maintain good governance. The Political Office wielded considerable influence and became a powerful player in determining the course of developments in this country.

Our arrival coincided with the beginning of the pro-democracy movement in Sikkim, which would eventually overthrow the monarchy. The political climate in Sikkim was becoming volatile, with pro-democracy protestors growing more vociferous each day and openly challenging the Chogyal's leadership. The Chogyal himself was becoming deeply unhappy with India's growing role in his country's affairs. He envied his neighbour Bhutan, a country that had successfully retained its independent status, even becoming a member of the United Nations; the Chogyal dreamed the same for Sikkim. It was his idealism and ambition of wanting a separate identity for Sikkim that would clash with India's rising security concerns.

It was their ineluctable fate that the Chogyal and Gyalmo would become pawns in the game of diplomacy and realpolitik as it played out across this Himalayan kingdom.

There were always people dropping by our home, at all odd hours of the day and night. Our glass-paned front verandah, with its airy and bright view to our flower-filled garden, became a cosy hangout. Homesick army officers who yearned for a slice of home would come over for my mother's home-cooked meals and end up playing cards till late into the night. Local politicians would often come unannounced and sip tea for hours. The discussions would become heated when radical leaders would visit, their political passion igniting our home.

One morning, I woke up to the voice of Kazi Lhendup Dorji, the charismatic leader of the Sikkim National Congress, the main opposition party, who was venting his anger and frustration with the monarchy. "The mood is very angry, Sir!" the soft-spoken leader told my father. Kazi led the anti-Chogyal faction and believed that the rights of the common people, Nepalese as well as the Lepchas and Bhutias, had been denied for too long. He accused the Chogyal of being autocratic and out of touch with the new realities, holed up in his palace. Kazi's voice grew sharper as he spoke about the urgent need for democratic reform of Sikkim's political system. Kazi himself belonged to the upper caste Bhutias who were Buddhist and of Tibetan descent. Along with the Lepchas, they were the original inhabitants of Sikkim who constituted 25 percent of the population, while the rest were of Nepalese descent.

Another frequent visitor to our home was Nar Bahadur Khatiawada, the twenty-year-old president of the Youth Congress, the dynamic youth leader who was rousing the masses with his fiery speeches.

Sometimes, if they saw me, Kazi and Bahadur would stop to talk to me, and would be very amused when I conversed with them in fluent Nepali.

My father was fully aware that he was under the Chogyal's

scrutiny at all times, and that by hosting the anti-establishment fellows in his home, he was provoking the ire of the palace. Yet my father couldn't help but like the soft-spoken Chogyal, with whom he had interacted on many a social occasion, both at the palace as well as at the Political Office. Whenever the Chogyal travelled to India, which he did by helicopter, it was my father who would see him off and receive him at the helipad, as part of the protocol arrangement between the Political Office and the palace.

In the midst of the political storm, the Chogyal's dignity remained unwavering and his humility, endearing. My mother too was charmed by the Chogyal, and recalled how she had once danced with him at a party. "A very nice man, a true gentleman," she relished the memory.

When my sister was born, the entire house went into a whirl of excitement following a phone call from the palace informing my father that the Chogyal wanted to come over to personally bless the baby on the occasion of the naming ceremony! In accordance with Maharashtrian custom, my mother whispered the name in the baby's ear, while my sister slept blissfully in a crib decorated with fresh mogra and marigolds, oblivious to the pandemonium around her. The ladies sang songs and distributed sweets. Amid the guests was the Chogyal, who appeared without much fuss at all, and presented my mother with a beautifully embroidered Sikkimese blanket for my baby sister. A small group consisting of my parents and their friends hovered around him, as he sipped tea, and appeared in no great hurry to leave, enjoying the warmth and hospitality heaped on him by all the guests in our home.

The sabre-rattling between China and India continued to intensify. The Chinese were incensed with what they perceived as India's aggression in the subcontinent, and were convinced the Soviets had helped India defeat Pakistan in the 1971 war. The Indo-Soviet Friendship Treaty that the two countries had signed just before the war had further angered them. The Chinese stance was raising hackles in New Delhi, which became very watchful of enemy activity, especially along the long border the two shared.

India had, over the years, reinforced the number of troops at strategic passes like Nathu La and Jelep La, which overlooked Chumbi Valley, a narrow strip of land that connects India to the northeast part of the country. There were rumblings of Chinese activity in Chumbi Valley, which lay perilously close to the Siliguri Corridor, and that was making Indian security officials extremely nervous.

In neighbouring Sikkim, meanwhile, things appeared quiet and calm, but under the surface, resentment against the Chogyal was mounting.

Trouble that had been brewing between the majority pro-democracy elements and the palace began to snowball, as demands for political reform in Sikkim grew noisier and cascaded into an avalanche in April 1973. Hundreds of demonstrators gathered at the Gangtok Stadium led by Kazi and other opposition groups, accusing the palace of rigging the recent elections and demanding that the Chogyal step down.

"End of the monarchy!" they shouted and their chants reverberated across the valley and around our house, where my mother, my sister and I were holed up, until calm was restored. As protests grew louder, the Political Office deputed my father to tour the country to assess the situation on the ground.

He left quietly one evening in a jeep, just he and his driver, and drove to Namchi, Geyzing and several other towns in the southern and western parts of Sikkim that were politically restive, where houses had been burned, shops looted and destroyed. We lost complete touch with our father, except for an occasional word from the Political Office that he was safe. To our immense relief, he returned three days later, his face lined with fatigue and distress. The currents were all too powerful. My father could feel the tide sweeping him off his feet. History was being shaped in front of his eyes, and we were smack in the middle of it.

Soon thereafter, Hope Cooke left for New York, taking her two children with her. She would never return to Sikkim again.

---

Ultimately, the Chogyal had little choice but to concede that the situation in Sikkim was out of control. He turned to the Indian Government to help restore law and order and on May 8, 1973, the Chogyal signed the document that would give India power over his country's destiny. In the general election that followed a year later, Kazi's Sikkim Janata Congress Party won by a thumping majority and formed the new government. New Delhi now had the man they wanted in the driver's seat.

In 1975, history was made when the people of Sikkim voted overwhelmingly for merging their country with India. The Indian Army would disarm the palace guards, the Sikkim Assembly would call for merger with India and Sikkim would officially join the Indian Union, becoming the 22$^{nd}$ state of India.

My father had been requesting the Ministry for a transfer out of Sikkim for quite some time, but Delhi had been unable to find a replacement for him. No officer wanted a posting to Gangtok. We left Sikkim in the summer of 1974. I missed my school, Dorji, the rabbits in our backyard and the view of the Kanchendzonga from our kitchen window. The 'godforsaken' place had become my home.

---

I can feel its energy miles before I see it.

Our jeep lurches around yet another hairpin bend. I crane my neck and peer into the distance. There it is, sparkling in the valley below. The Teesta, saucy and fearless, racing through the countryside I know so well, its icy waters casting shimmering rainbow shadows across the mountainside.

Sighting the Teesta fills me with a daring and makes me want to shout out loud. Instead, I sing, at the top of my voice, in fluent Nepali, a language I have not spoken since I was seven years old.

*Author in Parc Bertrand, Switzerland, 1977*

## Brown Girl in the Ring

### SWITZERLAND
### *1976–1979*

## Geneva

We ran across a meadow, my sister and I, a la *The Sound of Music*, the majestic Alps towering enormous behind us. The meadows were full of flowers – purple, pink and yellow – and little wooden chalets lay hidden amid them in the distance. The beauty of nature was so overpowering, it made us behave silly and giggly, wanting to scream and dance. We twirled round like Julie Andrews and then raced full speed, tumbling into a heap in the grass, just beside a brook where my parents sat in a sunny patch, laughing as they watched our childish capers. Even the few cows grazing nearby seemed amused. My mother opened the picnic basket she had prepared and handed us little *pooris* with a flavourful potato vegetable, 'picnic *bhaji*' we called it, which we ate hungrily.

"It's not fair," said my mother, as she sipped her coffee.

"What's not fair?" I asked.

"That so much beauty should be concentrated in one country."

We felt guilty, that we should be here while our own country was heaving with turmoil.

"Sikkim was beautiful too, but in a wild way," said my father. "Nothing to beat the sight of the sun setting over Kanchendzonga."

I lay in bed, listening to the roar of a motorcycle speeding through the night. Inside the room, the heater was gurgling, the sound mysteriously unfamiliar. It was past midnight, but I was too wide-awake to sleep, captivated by the newness of my surroundings. I peered at the wallpaper, just a few inches from my nose, its turquoise blue paisley motifs glowing neon in the dark. We were in a city called Geneva. I kept saying the name to myself, *Ge-Ne-Va*, so lyrical, like the name of a flower.

On the other side of the room my four-year-old sister was fast asleep, tired out from the long travel. It had been a frenetic few weeks, packing up our small flat in Delhi, which had been home for two years after Sikkim. A decision made deep inside the interiors of the Ministry of External Affairs, South Block, by a senior bureaucrat had once again turned our lives upside down, except this time there was much elation about where we were headed. As soon as the Ministry announced my father's appointment to Switzerland, our household was euphoric, especially my mother, who was thrilled that her husband had finally managed to land us an 'A' posting.

A new world beckoned. It was difficult to fathom that just forty-eight hours ago, we were in blazing, sweltering Delhi, where power cuts routinely kept us in mosquito-infested darkness for days and where water would come and go at its own whim, and now, suddenly by a stroke of serendipity, we were in a country that defied even a blink of imperfection.

We left behind a dark land, fraught by turmoil. A few months earlier, Prime Minister Indira Gandhi had slapped Emergency rule across the vast country, suspending everyone else's powers except her own. Every day we would hear harrowing accounts of arrests, raids and censorship against those who dared oppose

Mrs Gandhi's authority. Against this backdrop, 'Going West' felt surreal, like it was all part of a golden dream.

When our plane glided down at Cointrin Airport, we looked out the windows thirsting for the very first sight of our brand new home. In the distance, snowy peaks ringed the horizon of a land so ethereal you wondered if you had mistakenly stumbled into a postcard. In this utopian land, water gushed from taps with great abundance and lights simply never went off. It was pristine clean, as if no human beings had ever walked this land. No spitting or urinating on the roads, no overflowing garbage piles, no lecherous men ogling at us and even at my mother. Here, food came from the heavens – chocolate, cheese and candy in rainbow wraps. Aparna and I were delirious with joy, and I kept pinching her, just to make sure *she* was real, *I* was real, that *we* were actually here.

---

Our new home was a cosy, three-bedroom apartment on 36, Rue de l'Athenee. While my parents had been forewarned about the cost of living in Switzerland, it was only after we arrived that we discovered how brutally expensive it was. The perennial grudge of Indian Foreign Service officers was the lack of money in foreign postings. It was almost like the government sent you to a fancy place and punished you for being there. But no one really dared complain. Who in their right mind would want to provoke the ire of some junior *babu* (official) sitting in MEA who could rightfully turn around and say, "*Arrey, itna complain kar rahe ho, to Dilli wapas aja, bacchu*" (if you're going to whine so much, I can get you right back to Delhi). Airing any grievances with Delhi was unthinkable, considering the Foreign Service was replete with stories about officers getting hauled back midway through their posting, especially from 'A' countries, and being replaced by someone else.

Ever so often, during our family ritual of dinner table discussions, my father would turn philosophical and tell us the experience and exposure we got in foreign countries was far more enriching than all the money in the world could buy. As a ten-year-old, I didn't really get that. Especially since the corollary to our financial woes was *my* education. There was no question of my going to any of the international schools in Geneva, including the American School, which many of the UN employees' and diplomats' children attended. They were too exorbitant and out of our league.

"The embassy has recommended Parc Bertrand School," my father told my mother. "It's a local public school, just ten minutes' walk from our house. In Switzerland, the local schools are financed by taxes, so they are free. Alka, just imagine, her schooling will be free!" My father looked hugely relieved.

But my mother looked worried. "Won't the medium of instruction be French?" she asked.

"Alka, obviously it will be," said my father impatiently. "It's a Swiss school. But don't worry, I'm very sure the girls will pick it up fast, and anyway, it's good for them to learn French, it's a useful language." My father's mind had already moved on to important work matters. That I would adjust and learn a new language was axiomatic, not discussed for more than ten minutes at our dinner table.

Two weeks later, my mother and I set off to my new school, on the longest ten-minute walk in the history of my ten years.

The primary school was nestled in the heart of Parc Bertrand, one of the city's largest public parks, named after a wealthy Swiss couple, the Bertrands, whose ownership of the estate and surrounding gardens could be traced back to the seventeenth century. They later donated their property to the city of Geneva, which then converted the heritage house into a primary school. I was disinterested in the history of the garden, the flowers and the trees my mother was busy admiring. As we walked through the park, my only awareness was the acute pounding in my heart and the sensation that my legs did not belong to me. As we crossed manicured flower beds, my mother spoke to me enthusiastically, trying to distract me from my thoughts and to boost my spirits up. I was tempted to turn around and run right back to our house, the fluttering in my stomach was beginning to make me nauseous.

"Don't worry, you will make friends, you always settle in quickly. I'm sure you will like your new school," my mother said, hoping her cheerful tone would ease my anxiety. It just made me more sullen. I missed Rohini, my best friend in grade three at CJM, the Convent of Jesus and Mary, my school in Delhi. From sharing tiffin to eating orange lollies at the Kwality ice cream stall outside the school gate, to singing together on stage, side by side, in our school's year-end play, both Rohini and I were inseparable. She was the one who taught me how to hide our lunch boxes from the eagles that would sweep across the school courtyard to snatch away our food. The day I broke the news to her that I would be leaving, midway through third grade, we both cried and pledged we would write to each other every month. She would go on to grade four without me; I was jealous that she would soon find herself a new best friend and forget me, while I would be trapped with unfriendly strangers. Rohini felt so far away. Would I ever see her again? Would I ever have another best friend? My heart ached as we approached the school building.

The principal welcomed us in broken English. She was polite and matter-of-fact and told my mother she could accommodate me in grade four. The primary school education continued until grade five, she explained, after which most children attended the Lycée.

"As you may know, we do all the core subjects here in our school, as regulated by the Swiss public school system. Even though each canton has its own curriculum, we are required to teach the basic subjects, like history, social sciences, mathematics…"

"All in French?" asked my mother, trying to conceal her distress.

"Yes of course," said the principal. "French is the local national language in this part of Switzerland. After grade five, children must study a second local language; most of the children here choose German."

My mother glanced sideways at me, but my mind was still on Rohini and my friends in CJM. It was a good thing I wasn't paying too much attention to their conversation.

"Is there a uniform in your school?" my mother asked.

"No, no," the principal shook her head. "Schools in Switzerland do not have uniforms." She looked almost affronted by the thought.

"So, I will take your daughter to her classroom now," she said briskly and turned to me. "You can say goodbye to your mother."

My heart sank.

"I'll pick you up in a few hours, right outside the gate," my mother said to me with a forced brightness. "Wait for me there, don't go anywhere till I come." She patted my head, pretending not to see my eyes filled with dread, and waved to me as I followed the principal down a long hallway to my classroom. The fourth grade teacher was a large, strapping woman with a cherubic face and slightly crooked teeth. Madame Excoffier had very pink cheeks and lips, and a curly mop of boyish hair, and she didn't speak a single word of English! And to my utter dismay, neither did any of the fifteen children sitting in the classroom, staring at me standing in the doorway. As I stood there, I was hit by an even more disturbing realisation. *I was the only brown person there*. In fact, I was the *only* brown person in the *entire* school.

Boney M seemed to have written their just-released blockbuster single, *Brown Girl In the Ring*, just for me.

I looked down at the floor and wished it would open up and swallow me right there in my four-and-a-half-foot entirety. I thought of how my mother had taken me shopping the week before in Delhi, to buy me dresses and shoes because everything would be too expensive for us in Geneva. The dress I was wearing, which had looked pretty on me when I'd tried it on in an overcrowded clothing store in Delhi's Connaught Place shopping complex, felt all wrong now, with its frilly border and lacy sleeves. I felt ridiculously overdressed, like I was going to a party instead of school. Even my black shoes, which I had liked so much back home looked too shiny here. And why hadn't I noticed the bows on them before? I saw that most of the kids were wearing boots and jeans. I felt hot with embarrassment.

"Come in, come in, sit down," said Madame Excoffier in French, waving me towards an empty chair in the front row. She stumbled over my name as she introduced me to the class and went off into a stream of French, while fifteen pairs of eyes looked at me. Some kids giggled at my name. For the rest of the day, I only heard French all around me. How was I ever going to learn this language, which sounded like a whole lot of throat scratching going on? A few of the kids nodded at me, but no one really made any attempt to speak to me, I was the *fille Indienne* who didn't speak French.

During break, Madame Excoffier called out to one of the girls who had been sitting next to me, Isabel, and asked her to show me around. Isabel was so beautiful I couldn't take my eyes off her. I immediately thought of 'Heidi' as I looked at her. She had a thick golden braid and speckled green eyes. We made sincere efforts to communicate, but gave up after a whole lot of sign language. She showed me the bathrooms and ran off to join her friends, leaving me to battle a horrible loneliness that was creeping up my throat. There was no concept of learning support back then, which could have facilitated my easing into this very foreign environment. One was expected to learn via deep immersion. It was more like deep sea diving in the night.

The whole week went by, where I simply sat in class, drawing a blank, despite my efforts to keep track of words I might have heard before. A few of the kids had started greeting me with a *salut!* in the morning, including Isabel, and some others who would smile politely. Kids from the other classes continued to stare at me, like I was a centrepiece in a museum. I hated recess, because that was the time everyone headed out, giggling and gossiping, and formed tight little clusters that seemed impossible to infiltrate. Not that I even wanted to. I was far too intimidated to venture near them, and the prospect of being rejected was worse than sitting alone in the classroom. During lessons, Madame Excoffier would nod at me encouragingly, point to the blackboard and rattle off in gibberish again. History, geography, science and grammar all blurred into one huge mass. I could only distinguish one subject from another from the pictures in the textbooks.

There were only two other 'foreigners' in the school: Nakissa, an Iranian, and Rose, who was Vietnamese. To me, they didn't seem 'foreigners' like *I* was. Nakissa was very fair-skinned and blended seamlessly into the sea of white. Rose's parents had immigrated to Switzerland when she was very little and she spoke and acted more Swiss than even those around her. I realised I was observing everyone's skin tone obsessively. I thought back to my school in Delhi. Even there, the girls with fair skin were considered the pretty ones. They fell into three categories: *gori* meaning fair, *savli* was 'wheat complexioned' and *kali* was dark. The doomsday scenario was for girls to be *kali*. I wondered what they would have thought of Isabel. She would surely have won the part of Rapunzel in our school play last year.

Every morning I would wake up and make excuses not to go to school. It exasperated me that my mother didn't understand the depth of my malaise. She wasn't one to analyse herself sick over what her children said or didn't say, being more focused on the nitty-gritties of the chores and tasks she had on hand. So I learned to be emotionally self-sufficient, to fight the demons on my own, even as they played havoc with my self-worth. I figured that reaching school too early when everyone was congregated in the playground was not in my best interest – that was High Visibility. Instead, I perfected the art of walking in just as the bell rang, so I could go straight to the classroom. Low Visibility. I would quickly slink into my chair and focus on my next nightmare – trying to make sense of what everyone was saying.

I longed for the day when I could speak rapid-fire French like Madame Excoffier.

Getting accepted at school was going to be a lot harder as I discovered a few weeks later. It happened during recess. The November morning was crisp, and I shivered slightly. My coat felt thin and inadequate. I was the only one wearing a woollen cap. My mother had insisted on it. The weather was turning cold and she didn't want me getting sick, she said.

As I stood there at the edge of the playground, looking at the children playing on the swings, someone came running behind me and yanked my cap off. That same big boy I had noticed in my class who kept snickering at me. He tossed my hat to another boy as I ran towards him to retrieve it. The two boys kept tossing it back and forth, laughing at me as I tried to grab my cap back. A few more boys and girls joined them and the circle widened as they passed my cap around.

"*Les Indiens, tu pues!*" the boy said, and held his nose. Everyone laughed loudly. He held the cap away from his face and made more faces.

"*Ouais*," said another girl and screwed her face. "*Vachement mal.*"

You Indians stink. You're so dirty.

I saw Isabel walking towards us. She pushed her way through the small crowd that had gathered around me. "*C'est pas cool, ca,*" she scolded the boys and took my arm. "*Allez, viens avec moi,*" she said. Hurt and humiliation clogged my throat; I pushed back angry tears. I felt a rush of gratitude towards Isabel. I didn't know what the boys had said, but I knew it had been deeply insulting.

"*Merci beaucoup,*" I said to her. She nodded and offered me chewing gum.

The next day I forced my mother to take me shopping. I bought a pair of jeans, boots and a jacket, a tiny first step towards integration.

※

In the seventies, Switzerland was a deeply conservative society, cold and unwelcoming to foreigners, and determined to keep their beautiful land to themselves. The immigration history of Switzerland reflected a predominantly Swiss society, with early immigrants from neighbouring countries like Italy, particularly after the Second World War, when Switzerland needed workers for their factories, railways and road building, to fill the labour shortage for infrastructural projects. The country had strict immigration laws in effect, which clearly stated the terms and conditions for these guest workers and their status in Switzerland. This icy policy towards foreigners only began to shift slightly in the eighties, with improved efforts to assimilate foreign workers and refugees and encourage adoptions from poor countries. Pressure from the left groups led to a greater thrust towards integration and naturalisation of existing foreigners.

But during the period of our posting, there was a strong sweeping sense of identity and pride in being Swiss, with far-right politicians pushing for legislation to limit the number of foreigners in the country. The message was clear: foreigners, especially from Third World countries like ours, were not welcome. It was only many years later as an adult that I would learn that Switzerland had experienced a peak of xenophobia then, coinciding with the years that we were there. Of course I didn't need history textbooks to corroborate what I had experienced first-hand.

Underneath the pureness lay the debris of racism. Like the snow surrounding me, it numbed me, at first just the fingers and toes, then the nose, and gradually it crept into the entire body and mind, till a deep freeze set in which would take several years to thaw. In my sheltered existence in which I had so far only experienced affection – from my immediate and extended family of grandparents, uncles, aunts and cousins, who would shower us with love whenever we went back to India on home leave – the world lurking outside the doors of our apartment felt alien and cold. A feeling of inferiority was seeping in, inflicting scars on my self-esteem that would remain seared into my consciousness for much of my formative life.

My parents, luckily for them, were free from the angst that I was drowning in. Wrapped in nationalism from head to toe, they hobnobbed with other diplomats and dignitaries, proudly wore their national dress, ate Indian food and listened to Indian classical music. They didn't have the peer pressure we had, as kids. No one was going to tell *them* that Indians smelled bad or were dirty, which we heard routinely from white kids.

---

That's when the migraines started.

The first time I got a headache, I tried to dismiss it, thinking it would go away if I ignored it. I had come home from school and was longing to curl up on the sofa and read Enid Blyton's *Five Go to Demon's Rocks*. Soon my headache became so persistent I had to lie down. I closed my eyes, but the pounding increased, no matter which way I turned my head. The pain seemed to be concentrated on one side. When I opened my eyes, I could see only half of the room, the other was in shadows. By this time my head felt like it was going to burst and I threw up violently.

The next day we went to see Dr Borgeaux, who, after examining me, said, "Migraine is a sign of puberty. Do you have your period?"

"But she's only ten-and-a-half," exclaimed my mother.

"Well, she's going to get her period early. Is she having a lot of stress?"

My mother looked at me. I looked back at her and shook my head. "No," I lied. Prevarication seemed easier than launching into explanation.

Dr Borgeaux was right. A few weeks later, I got my first period. Now I had to deal with a double headache – migraines *and* periods.

---

My father finally came to terms with the extra expense, realising it was rather fanciful on his part to expect his daughter to conquer a new language simply by sitting in the classroom, without external reinforcement. A hunt for a French tutor began.

We were referred to a Madame Donici, an octogenarian French lady who had decided that in her old age, teaching poor foreigners from Third World countries would be a noble thing. So she took it upon herself to educate me in the fine nuances of the scratchy-throat language with a vim that was hard to pin to her skeletal frame. When I couldn't understand the past passé of the verb *chanter*, I would count the wrinkles on her forehead and marvel at how so many could fit in the narrow space between her eyebrows and her hairline. She would never forget to wear her make-up, the brightest red lipstick and curly thick mascara. Every time I entered her over-decorated, wallpapered candled home I felt like I was stepping into a fifteenth-century Renaissance painting. Everything about Madame Donici felt a hundred years old, but she was a dogged teacher who helped me conquer the forbidding realm of *plus-que-parfait, subjonctif* and *imparfait* in every verb I could possibly need. Madame Donici's rigorous coaching taught me to appreciate the nuances of the verb, the intricacies of conjugation. Every time we completed a verb, she shared my exaltation, and within six months, I was able to study math, history and science with a fluency in French that surpassed even my English. And of course, added to that were all the slang words I acquired in school and I was swearing *merde* like a local.

The most exciting part of tuition at Madame Donici's was the bakery I crossed, on Route de Florissant, where I would spend several minutes staring at the fine display of candy and cakes on the shelves. In the end, I would always choose the same, sugar-powdered doughnut, which had a juicy strawberry filling that sent me into raptures, and the thought of eating that doughnut was the only reason that made tuition sufferable.

Gradually, the big bolted door that stood between me and the French-speaking world began to yield. Within a few months it swung open and to my delight, I was able to walk right through to the other side. To my enormous relief I found the world on the other side to be less sinister than I had envisaged it to be. Learning the language was the best solution to my lack of confidence, and the day I actually understood Madame Excoffier's explanation about the Bastille was a *bingo!* moment. In six months' time, Madame Excoffier pronounced me fully proficient in French. It made me realise that while I could never overcome the obstacle of *looking* different, at least I'd pole-vaulted the language barrier, which accorded me a far more generous degree of acceptability amongst my peers. In language class, I wrote my first poem titled *l'etang* (the pond). Madame Excoffier was so pleased with it, she made me read it aloud in class. It was a turning point. For the first time since I landed in Switzerland, I felt empowered.

---

My sister and I became chubby. All those pastries and chocolate, milk and cheese were having their effect. In fact, I began to notice two little mounds sticking out of my chest.

"Breasts," my mother said to me one day. "We'd better go buy you a bra."

I felt utterly self-conscious about my new body and I hated that it was growing up without my consent. While some of the girls in my class were big built, most were not wearing bras yet.

"I hate them," I told my mother one day.

"What?"

"Breasts," I said, feeling shy to even say the word.

My mother smiled and, trying to sound reassuring, said, "You should feel proud of them; boys like them."

I was aghast that my mother would ever say such a thing to me. I stared at her in horror, made a face and ran out of the room.

---

My sister, who had adjusted well to her pre-school, was too young to be a companion to me. She was my mother's little shadow who snitched on me and got me into trouble. Six years older than Aparna, I was the bully sister who made her cry. I was also a sulky thirteen-year-old, angry most of the time. I sought refuge in writing. Most of all, I liked being alone. Being in my room allowed me to cut off the outside world, for which I had little empathy.

I plastered my room from floor to ceiling with posters – Boney M, Abba, Charlie's Angels, Bee Gees, Wonder Woman, Grease, alongside my favourite Hindi film stars. French pop stars were hugely popular in Geneva back then and like most Swiss teenagers, I adored them. France Gall, Chantal Goya, Joe Dassin, Sylvie Vartan, Sheila B Devotion filled up my life with their music of love and longing. From my pre-teen standpoint, they were non-judgemental; because I did not believe they were capable of discriminating, I placed them on a pedestal. My other favourite was the Spanish female duo Baccara who were revving up the charts across Europe with their blockbuster hit, *Yes Sir, I Can Boogie*. They were sassy and sexy and I would sing their songs at the top of my voice

It was odd that I should find solace in a space far removed from my day-to-day existence. Hindi cinema. Thanks to the Diplomatic Bag, we got our steady supply of film magazines – *Stardust*, *Star & Style* and *Filmfare*, from which I would diligently cut out posters and lovingly adorn my walls with them. As a result, I had giant cut-outs of glamour queens Parveen Babi and Zeenat Aman, the charismatic Rishi Kapoor-Neetu Singh smiling down at me from my walls.

The Indian community in Geneva was small, but highly enthusiastic about watching movies from back home. The enterprising ones found a small theatre in the outskirts of Geneva, which agreed to screen Hindi films once a month. That's how I saw all the iconic movies of that period – *Ghar, Amar Akbar Anthony, Parvarish, Muquaddar Ka Sikandar, Trishul, Badaltey Rishtey, Hum Kisise Kum Nahin, Yadon Ki Baraat, Khel Khel Mein* – sitting in the cushy confines of a darkened cinema hall in Geneva. My parents had cassettes of the latest songs, duly recorded by relatives back home, which would accompany us on our drives through the Jura Mountains and lakes of Switzerland. We called them the 'Jura songs' – *Chura Liya, O Saathi Chal, Tujho Mere Sur Mein, Lekar Hum Deewana Dil, Ek Mein Aur Ek Tu, Yeh Mera Dil, Jaaneman Jaaneman* and scores of other timeless melodies. It was the heyday of the Asha Bhosle-RD Burman musical creativity and the magic of their songs cast a permanent spell on my impressionable mind. Through Hindi movies, I allowed myself to drift off into a world that felt familiar and comforting. Thus, like many others of my generation, I grew up with Bollywood melodies lingering in my consciousness, each song evoking a collective wave of nostalgia and memories.

It took my parents by surprise when they discovered I could sing. One evening we were at Uncle Chopra's house for a party and, after dinner, a few people were asked to sing, including my mother who rendered a Marathi song in her lilting, melodious voice. Everyone gave her an admiring applause when, suddenly, Uncle Chopra, a gregarious Punjabi who worked for GATT, turned to me and said, "Ashwini, your turn, I'm sure you can sing very well." I liked Uncle Chopra and his wife Pooja, with whom we would sometimes go cross-country skiing on weekends.

"Mother can, surely daughter can too!" said Pooja Aunty.

"She hasn't shown much interest, I haven't heard her sing," said my mother. To be fair, my mother had, on a few occasions tried to teach me Indian classical music. She would bring out her *tanpura* and make me practise the notes of Raag Yaman, but I would be disinterested. Tonight, both my parents were taken aback by my uncharacteristic enthusiasm.

"I can sing," I said. "Hindi songs."

"Really?" asked my mother in surprise. "Which one?" she said, trying not to sound doubtful.

"From *Sholay*," I said.

I started singing the raunchy *Mehbooba Mehbooba* and rendered it from beginning to end, all three stanzas, with great vigour and in perfect tune. I ended it with a flourish and a bow and waited for the applause. There was a stunned silence and then everyone broke into loud cheers, my father clapping me on my back, my mother looking speechless and my sister – the only one privy to my bedroom singing – smiling cheekily, the Keeper of the Big Secret.

"*Arrey waah,*" boomed Uncle Chopra. "*Beta,* you sing so well, one more, one more." So I sang another of my favourites, *Yeh Raatein Nayee Purani,* from *Julie*. From then on, uncles and aunties would regularly make me sing the latest Hindi film songs at parties.

---

I lived in two worlds. The world of Indians and the one populated by the Swiss. The minute I walked out the door, I threw off my Indian culture as fast as I could, like extra clothing, along with its smells, language, food and music. Lata Mangeshkar and Kishore Kumar who ruled in the house, were quickly replaced by Chantal Goya and France Gall as I walked down Route de Florissant to school. I loved them equally, with as much ardour, but I kept them separate, like salt and pepper jars.

I was prudish, but I secretly read Harold Robbins, which I found buried deep inside my parents' bookshelf and felt the blush of shame and excitement at discovering a world that no one ever talked about in Indian homes.

---

It was difficult to ignore the beauty that surrounded us. We would spend Sunday afternoons at the lake – the sapphire blue Lac Léman which stretched out like the sea into the horizon. Aparna and I would peer at the misty distance where water met the sky, pretending we could see Montreaux at the other end. On a clear day, the Alps would rise out of the lake, like a snowy apparition. The four of us would walk around the lakeside; my mother would eat her favourite pista ice cream, while my sister and I would get the three-tiered rocket sticks, chocolate at the tip, vanilla in the centre and orange at the bottom, and compete with each other on who could finish it without dripping.

The Jet d'Eau was an awesome sight – the fountain rose high in the sky, scattering rainbow hues around it. My sister and I would squint to look at its tip and squeal with excitement when we got drenched. Clutching bread in our hands, we would stand at the edge of the lake and wait in great excitement for the flock of ducks to come up close. Then we would shower them with breadcrumbs. There would always be one duckling, the laggard, that wasn't quick enough to snatch the crumbs, watching the others eat its share. My sister would always save some bread in her pocket for the less fortunate duck. The altruistic streak in her was strong even when she was just five years old.

The outing on the lake was a charmed memory of our Geneva posting. Lac Leman, the Jet d'Eau and the flower clock were the three jewels in the crown of our Sunday family outings. Not far from the lake was the magnificent Palais de Nations, the European headquarters of the United Nations, a powerful presence in this small city, where it had its second largest office outside New York. Several countries had offices dedicated to United Nations affairs in Geneva, including India, which had its Permanent Mission (PMI) that dealt exclusively on matters pertaining to the UN.

The Emergency made India the *enfant terrible* of the international community. It was the talking point for all diplomats and UN officials whenever they met officers from the Indian embassy or PMI. My father and the Ambassador maintained an official response, but privately were extremely distraught by reports of worsening conditions they were getting from back home. Prime Minister Indira Gandhi, in an attempt to consolidate her own power, had invoked Article 352 of the Indian Constitution that allowed her to crush fundamental rights – civil liberties – in what would later be seen as the worst distortion of democracy in India since independence. The postponing of elections, silencing of the media and the rumours of torture of protestors made representing India a very delicate responsibility for both my father and the Ambassador. It was not the most ideal time to be defending one's country, my father would privately complain to my mother.

"The situation in India is really grim," said my father when he came home one evening, his face flushed and agitated.

"What's happening? It can't get worse than what it already is," said my mother while feeding my sister a few bites of *chapati*, as she sat at the dining table, colouring with crayons. I was curled up in my usual spot on the sofa near the window, immersed in Darrell Rivers' adventures at Malory Towers.

"Sanjay Gandhi is going around forcibly sterilising people! He is wreaking havoc, apparently, pulling people off the streets, literally, sterilising people indiscriminately."

"How can he do this, can't the PM stop her own son?" asked my mother, looking shocked.

"Apparently not," said my father. "That such a thing can happen is a complete travesty. The Swiss Foreign Minister asked us about it today, it was so embarrassing and painful to have to explain this. Sanjay Gandhi's not sparing anyone, old people, young married men, women; it's craziness."

"How long is the Emergency going to go on?" my mother asked. "People are suffering enough."

"I wish I had an answer," sighed my father. "One thing is for sure, Mrs Gandhi has frittered away all her goodwill and will likely lose the elections."

The Emergency would go on for twenty-one months. Through letters from relatives, we would get news about the gloom – the shortages and the hardships. And sure enough, when it was lifted, Indira Gandhi lost the elections, the biggest loss the Congress Party would face since independence.

---

In Geneva, my father's prime responsibility included disarmament, a specialised, political portfolio of complex issues such as nuclear, chemical and conventional weapons. India's Peaceful Nuclear Explosion, the PNE, conducted two years previously, in 1974, did not make his job easier, as it was constantly brought up in conferences at the UN and other international forums. There was a hostility directed towards Indian officials, as if their country had betrayed the global equilibrium by conducting the PNE. It was up to my father and the Ambassador to present India's case at the United Nations, which they would do earnestly and passionately.

My father's patriotism towards his country wrapped him tightly from head to toe. Any advancements India made, particularly its breakthroughs in science, would be a source of great pride to him. When India conducted its underground nuclear explosion in a Rajasthan desert, my father believed it heralded India's status as a major power on the world stage. To him, the PNE had stunned the world because it showcased India's nuclear capability.

"The application potential of nuclear technology for developing countries like India is immense," said my father. "Mining, agriculture, electricity, deep excavation and medicine will all benefit from nuclear energy, which China has already embarked on a decade before us." That Western countries and China did not treat India on par was a source of great frustration for my father. "Double standards," he would say. "First the NPT and now, after our PNE, the West is treating us like a pariah nation."

---

Lately, I had taken to collecting snails on my way back from school. There were so many in Parc Bertrand that one day I collected a whole lot of them in a box and brought them home. Much to my disappointment, when I woke up the next morning, they had all disappeared. My mother said they must have wandered out of the open windows. My sister and I were heartbroken.

"They are outdoor creatures," my mother consoled us. "It's not fair to box them in."

The snails I had hoped to keep as pets in a small cardboard box in our living room were among the multitude of memories I have about Switzerland, which became our home at a formative period in my life – the transition from childhood to adolescence. It was also a time when my sister and I started to become friends. The six-year age difference between us began to feel less of a yawning gap by the time she turned seven, in the final year of our Geneva posting. Preoccupied with my own inner turmoil for the better part of our stay, I had not really noticed the precocity in Aparna. A serious child, she would often surprise us by the things she said, because they were so mature and sensible. My mother said she forgot sometimes that her second child had only just turned seven. One afternoon, I saw Aparna poring over my father's Foreign Service Directory.

"Why are you reading that?" I asked her in surprise.

"I thought maybe I can find out where we are getting posted to next," she said.

As the two-and-a-half-year mark approached, we began guessing which country we would be headed to next. This would become our favourite game over the years. The Game of Names, predicting *Where To Next?* Aparna's fascination with the world of the Foreign Service started in Geneva and even though she herself never joined the civil services, that didn't stop her from spending hours leafing through the directory, which she studied in meticulous detail, much to my father's amusement.

Our time in Geneva was short-lived. Thanks to our dinner table discussions, we were vaguely aware of the machinations that were taking place among envious contenders back in Delhi.

A posting to Geneva was so coveted that once you got there, the goal was to stick around as long as you could.

"Go anywhere, but don't go to Burma," joked Uncle Mani, a friend of my father's who had visited the country a few times on UN assignments. Alas, his words turned out to be prophetic.

---

Our last winter was heavy with sentimentality. Even though no posting order had come as yet, we knew with certainty that it would be our final winter there. Noses against the window, frosting the panes, Aparna and I looked out of our 36, Rue de l'Athénée living room as soft flakes fell, the sight of first snow. The Christmas tree glowed in the corner, sprinkling us with its warm lights, reminding us of its presence, one that would become a December fixture in our homes through our lives, no matter which part of the world we lived in.

Closed-door conversations between my parents were the first sign that something was brewing. There was change in the air; both Aparna and I could sniff it. One night after dinner, my sister and I stood with our ears to the bedroom door, listening to my parents speaking in low voices. My father suddenly opened the door and was surprised to see us.

"Why aren't you sleeping?" he asked us. From his drawn face, we immediately sensed something was wrong. We both trooped into their room and plopped onto their bed. My mother was sitting at her dressing table, her face small and pinched.

"Girls, we are getting posted," said my father.

There was silence.

"To Burma," said my mother in a tearful voice.

My sister and I looked at them, trying to process the news. We had never heard of Burma, but from the expression on our parents' faces, it was obviously not a great place to be heading to.

"Where is that?" I asked nervously.

"It's next to India," said my mother. "A poor country, very very backward."

My sister and I looked alarmed. A pall of depression was descending on us, slowly and steadily, as we absorbed the significance of this announcement. Even though we always knew in the back of our minds that leaving Geneva was imminent, we weren't prepared to start all over again, so soon, just as we'd started to feel settled.

"You should have tried to get a UN job," said my mother looking at my father resentfully. "So many of our officers have done that in Geneva. Why can't you try?"

My father did not reply. He knew he could offer no palliative to the shock inflicted on his family. There was simply nothing but stoic acceptance that could counter this blow. It was the Ministry's unwritten code: you went from good to bad. But why did they have to fling you from good to worse? There was no denying my mother's angst; there were innumerable examples of Indian government officers who had managed to wrangle UN jobs or get posting extensions to stay on in Geneva after their assignments. But this was something my father would never entertain. To grovel before someone higher up in the Ministry to request a review of the posting order went against everything he stood for. My father believed no matter where he was sent to represent his country, he would go, head held high. It was his duty to serve his country and whether it was Switzerland or Burma, he would do so with the highest level of pride and dedication. Asking headquarters to change his posting would be casting a black mark on his integrity. He felt torn and distressed, as he looked at the three crestfallen faces in front of him.

"Look, it won't be so bad, Alka," he finally said.

"Ravi, you know it's going to be terrible," said my mother, bitterly. "Why does the Ministry always do this to us? They sent us from Washington to Sikkim and now from here to another godforsaken place! Ravi, it's because we have no contacts in the Ministry, no godfather. This is the price we have to pay."

My father said nothing. My sister and I looked at each other in dismay. Our future looked uncertain and bleak.

"Mom, when do we have to leave?" I asked in a small voice. My mother was on the verge of tears. "In three months," she said.

My sister and I sat huddled together on my parents' bed, while my mother continued to speak of colleagues who had gone from one good posting to even better ones.

"Not everyone gets dumped from an 'A' country to a 'C'," she said. "Look at the Sinhas, they went from Brussels to Tokyo. And the Mehras went from Washington to Bonn! How did they manage that? And the Sarins, they went from Moscow to, to..."

"Netherlands," said my sister. We all looked at her stunned. "It was in Daddy's IFS book," she said and we all laughed, thankful to find something to break through the cloud of misery.

"Off you go to bed," said my mother. "And don't worry, girls, we will pull through, we always do! We are survivors!"

We went about our normal routines like zombies; sometimes I would forget we would be leaving Geneva, because despite all its shortcomings, it had become home. Then suddenly it would convulse me, like a fever. That soon my present would be part of a past and that past would become like a mirage.

Fearful of what lay ahead, my sister and I pieced together a picture of Burma as a forgotten land full of snakes and mosquitoes, where the weather would be hot like India, a country devoid of candy and cheese. The country we created in our minds was frighteningly close to the reality we would face in a few months' time.

The news that we were going to Burma spread quickly in the Indian community, which showered us with attention and solidarity in the last leg of our stay. A majority of them worked with GATT, WTO and UN organisations, jobs my mother was so envious of and wished my father could have considered. But she too knew that her husband's heart belonged to the Foreign Service and his commitment to it was like a blood relationship, and no matter how seductive the temptation, he would be unflinching in his loyalty towards his country.

The only information we had about Burma was from the Ministry; my father had spoken to his counterpart in the embassy in Rangoon to discuss various matters. We now had every reason to worry about the next stop on our Foreign Express.

---

She was tall and lanky, with warm brown eyes and dimples. We instantly hit it off in school. She belonged to my 'India World', a world I looked forward to unwinding in. I found the perfect companion in Darshini, a model adolescent, with no angst or anger, no rebellion or defiance. She behaved with the same equanimity with her parents as she did towards her friends. Deeply musical, she would spend hours strumming her guitar. When we got together, we would practise the latest pop songs;

one of our favourites was Abba's *Hasta Mañana*, which she would strum on her guitar and we would sing. Once, we were both to perform a Hindi duet in a Diwali programme. Just as we prepared to go on stage, Darshini got stage fright. She got nervous often, but this time, it paralysed her. I ended up singing the song solo, but I missed her being with me on stage.

We swam together in her building's pool on Route de Florissant. After our swim, we would troop upstairs, along with her brother, and drink large glasses of delicious chocolate milk. Except Darshini, who would not touch it, because she was grievously allergic to milk.

My chapter on Switzerland would be incomplete without a tribute to Darshini. She became one of my closest friends with whom I spent three beautiful years together. We spent many an afternoon letting our imaginations soar. That's how we created 'Daisy Dewdrops', an animation strip in which Daisy would fly around on a broomstick correcting the wrongs of the world. Darshini dreamed of a world filled with Daisy Dewdrops, she was that kind of a person, who believed in kindness and love. I penned my first book, 120 pages long, in Geneva, which she illustrated.

After I left Geneva, Darshini and I would never meet again.

Ten years later, she tragically succumbed to a massive asthma attack in a New York subway. My memories of her remain frozen from the time we both were twelve-year-olds, listening to *Cherry Pink* and imagining Daisy Dewdrops looking down on a golden land.

*Hasta Mañana* Darshini, *Till We Meet Again.*

*The author with her mother and sister in Maymyo (now known as Pyin Oo Lwin), Burma, 1981*

# Behind the Bamboo Curtain

## BURMA
*1979–1981*

## Rangoon

Forlorn and miserable, the four of us sat in the run-down lobby of a hotel in downtown Rangoon. Dad swatted at the flies while my sister and I looked ready to burst into tears. My mother's face looked drained. The heat was oppressive. Twenty-four hours ago we had been in God's country, drenched in plenty. Now we felt as if someone had locked us in a dungeon and thrown away the keys. My mother grumbled at Dad for not using enough 'pull' in Delhi to get his posting changed and we cursed both our parents for the misery we felt we didn't deserve.

After spending three years in Switzerland, the Land of Abundance, Burma felt like a wasteland. We hated our father's job that had hurled us from the epitome of luxury into this pit of penury. We had just spent a month in India on home leave at my grandmother's home in Pune, and now even India seemed like the far more advanced neighbour. Burma's doors were tightly shut to all foreigners, except a handful of embassy personnel that included us. There was the occasional Westerner, typically the backpacker coming through from Bangkok, who was given a maximum one-week visa to stay in Rangoon. Intellectuals and academics had fled, and those left behind were ruthlessly cowed into submission. We used to think it couldn't get worse than the Iron Curtain. We discovered the Bamboo Curtain was far worse. Our posting to Burma coincided with one of the darkest periods in the country's modern history.

We were in a country ruled by the military junta. Too young to fully absorb the gravity of the crisis outside the compound of our home, I was aware, through snatches of conversations adults had, that Burma was under the rule of a military dictator General Ne Win, who sealed off his country from the rest of the world, so that no one could question his authority. During his thirty-year rule, Burma virtually vanished from the world radar. Through his Burma Socialist Programme Party, Ne Win adopted a brand of socialism that pushed the nation to the brink of bankruptcy. The reclusive Ne Win may have achieved his goal of isolation by withdrawing from the international community and even the Non-Aligned Movement (NAM), which Burma had been a founding member of, but it was a Pyrrhic victory. A country that once boasted self-sufficiency in food and had championed democracy was now a basket case, one of the poorest in the world.

---

"Come on, what's taking you so long!" My sister carefully parted the branches of the jackfruit tree she had climbed, and called out to me, standing a few feet below. She had managed to haul herself a fair distance up the giant fruit tree, which occupied the far end of our garden. I could barely distinguish her face peering at me through the dozens of plump, spiky yellow-green orbs, dangling around her like ornaments on a Christmas tree.

I looked up at her, comfortably perched on a wide branch. Aparna was a certified tree climber, having explored nearly all of the ones in our garden.

"Hurry up! It's easy," she said.

I looked at her doubtfully. My balance was not half as good as hers. I began my ascent cautiously, refusing to look down till I found myself wedged on a solid flat branch next to Aparna, midway up the tree.

"Move over a bit," I nudged her.

"Hey, you almost pushed me off," she said crossly, and shifted to the side to make more space for me.

"Look at all these jackfruits!" I exclaimed. "They are enormous."

"And look at all the ants," said Aparna. "Hope they don't bite."

"They are black ants," I said, nervously scanning the branches, praying I wouldn't see any red ones.

"Let's hide otherwise Mama is going to find me," said my sister, looking worried. "I ran away without finishing my lunch."

"Why did you do that?" I scolded her. "You know she gets angry when you don't eat."

From our vantage point, we had a clear view of our small colonial-era cottage perched at the edge of a large overgrown garden full of jackfruit, durian, pomelo and banana trees. Located on Budd Road, our cottage was part of a cosy cluster of bungalows where Indian families from the embassy and defence services lived. In our compound, we were shielded from the reality of this dark land that lurked just a kilometre down the road. In its glory days, Budd Road must have been a splendid residential complex for British officers during their rule in Burma, but now it was derelict and poorly maintained with plumbing and piping that seemed to equally date back to those British times.

My sister and I heard the familiar jangle of bells that seemed to grow louder as it approached our compound. The street vendor was pushing his cart full of sweet and sour plums and berries, which we would often buy. We began to clamber down the tree to try and catch him before he left. Just then my mother walked into the garden and spotted us.

"Aparna, come here right now and finish your food!" I got thoroughly scolded for encouraging my sister to undertake such a dangerous tree-climbing expedition, even while I tried to tell her it had nothing to do with me. Brushing off my sister's pleas that she wasn't hungry, my mother whisked her inside to finish her half-eaten meal. "No berries for you," she said sternly.

The truth was my sister and I had lost our appetite ever since we arrived in Burma. We tried the milk from a local milkman, but it tasted so watery that my sister gagged and refused to drink it again. We were advised by others, who had been in Burma longer than us, not to drink the milk for fear of contamination. Equally, if not more worrying was the water, a source of many illnesses, including jaundice and hepatitis, which were rampant diseases in Rangoon. Within our first few weeks, there was also a heightened fear of plague because of rat infestation in the city. The impact of our transfer became almost immediately visible on my sister, who rapidly began losing weight and within a few months had shrunk several kilos; her chubby cheeks vanished and her face adopted a pallor. Her sunken, hollow eyes gave her the appearance of an old shrivelled woman and snatched away from her the bounce of a seven-year-old.

We felt completely isolated from the rest of the world in Rangoon. There was nothing to read, no books or magazines, and no television, so we would wait longingly for Fridays, when the Diplomatic Bag would arrive from India bursting with letters, newspapers and magazines. I would grab *Stardust* and *Star & Style*, and devour each and every page. I would eagerly look for the posters inside, which I'd then plaster across the walls of the room my sister and I shared. So there was Tina Munim, the new sensation who was creating waves in Bollywood, Rekha in a metamorphosed avatar looking the epitome of sophistication, the pink-cheeked Rishi Kapoor in *Karz*, Vinod Khanna, Amitabh Bachchan and my all-time favourite Dimple Kapadia, gazing down at us fondly from our walls. Once again, as I had done in Geneva, I created a sanctuary in my room, finding solace amid posters and Hindi music, which I played off a small cassette player.

The world of Abba, Charlie's Angels, snow, chocolate and white-skinned people who took pristine water, air and affluence for granted, seemed to belong to a far-off universe. Sometimes I wondered if our stay in Switzerland had been a dream because, as the months slipped by, the snow-clad country seemed more like a vision. Turning thirteen and catapulting into a new country simultaneously were not the best of combinations. I was experiencing puberty-related mood swings, drowning myself in self-pity and sulky silences. I thought of all my Indian friends who would continue to live in Geneva for the rest of their lives because their fathers worked in GATT or at the UN. I envied them fiercely and grumbled how lucky they were compared to us. I complained far more than my sister, always the more accommodating of the two of us.

"I wish we could go back to Geneva," I would tell my mother bitterly.

"I know, I wish I could too," my mother would sigh. "But don't worry, you will get used to it here."

"We are being punished for having enjoyed three-and-a-half years in Switzerland," my mother would complain to my father.

The dining table, as it had done in the past, would become

our citadel of knowledge about the country we lived in and the world beyond. Over meals, my father would give us insights into the political climate in Burma, but he was always cautious, even within the four walls of our home. "You never know who is listening," he would say. "One should not speak too openly about the government." Nevertheless, through his encounters with the locals, he would piece together a picture of a country that was slowly and quietly sinking into a morass.

"Alka, things have become so bad that they are now forced to import food," he told us one evening at the dinner table. "I won't be surprised if riots break out." We looked at him in dismay.

"I don't think it will happen right away," said my father looking at our scared faces. "But it is definitely brewing."

"How can Ne Win believe that economic progress is bad for the country?" asked my mother. "Michael and Sandra were telling me about their ancestral house and how one day, without any warning, the government just took away their property." Michael and Sandra were a local Burmese couple my mother had befriended. Many Burmese, even though they were Buddhist, had adopted Western names during the colonial British period.

"You better not encourage Michael and Sandra to come to our house," said my father, looking alarmed.

"It was so nice of them to take us on that picnic along Irrawaddy River," recalled my mother. "They are really very nice people."

"Any PTDPs happening?" my sister, who had been lost in thought, suddenly piped in. We all looked at her enquiringly.

"Postings, transfers, demotions, promotions?"

"Have you been going through the IFS Directory again?" asked my mother and we all laughed heartily.

My sister nodded. "Ya," she said dolefully. "To check if anyone is leaving Geneva, so that we can go back there again."

The four of us chuckled at her clever acronym, which aptly described the narrative of our nomadic lives. Secretly, how I wished her words would ring true, so we could go back to the dreamy land we had just left behind.

---

Once every six months, a ship would come from Penang in Malaysia, bringing a consignment of goodies from the outside world that embassy personnel were allowed to buy: cheese, butter, coffee, fragrant soaps, chocolate – foods that were ambrosia for us. My sister and I would fight over the shiny green 7UP cans, which we were allowed as a treat. I would drink mine quickly and bully my sister into giving me sips from hers. Many times she would disappear and hide until she had finished her entire can of 7UP, away from my grabbing hands.

My mother was right. Switzerland eventually receded into memory as the present took over the past. The durian trees in our garden became our friends, and spotting frogs inside our toilet bowls became a favourite activity for my sister and me. Gradually, we discovered beauty in this oppressed country. Soon the golden glow of the Shwedagon Pagoda replaced the tug of the Alpine meadows.

---

There was no regular school for me in Rangoon. Instead, a small three-room bungalow, cobbled together for children of foreigners, most of them from neighbouring Southeast Asian countries like Thailand and the Philippines, served as our learning ground. Because of the small numbers of students, three higher grades were clumped into one. I was the oldest in the school. Locals who had fluency in English had been granted special permission by the authorities to teach at this school, and it was considered a mark of privilege for them to be associated with foreigners. Once they entered the premises, they freely mingled with us, becoming more like friends than teachers. I was mesmerised by one particular teacher, Daw Mu Mu, who taught us history. She had her long hair tied in a neat bun and her flawless pearly skin smeared with a layer of *thanaka* – a cream from the bark of the thanaka tree which Burmese women and men alike applied to protect themselves from the harsh sun – gave her an ethereal glow. Daw Mu Mu's hair was legendary, a talking point among the girls, especially. We all hoped that one day her pin would fall and her hair would come cascading down to the floor. But the pin was unyielding, and her bun remained tightly in place.

*Author and her teachers, Burma, 1979*

Teacher Vicky, who taught math, loved to chat. She agreed to tutor me at home, a risk she willingly took. Pretty and plump, with short dark hair, crinkling eyes and dimples, she was animated and full of life, shedding her reserve the minute she entered our home. She would tell me stories from her childhood and adolescence, about growing up in a prosperous business family, about the boyfriends she had, the parties her parents would host. She would speak wistfully of her English-speaking cousins and friends who had fled Burma and never returned. Life was good back in the old days, she sighed. Now, everything had changed.

---

Sometimes my sister and I would accompany our mother into town. It was a disembodied experience, like stepping into a black and white picture. The modernity we had seen in Europe felt like part of a previous life. In some ways it might have been easier had we never experienced the luxury of clean air and water and modern living. Dilapidated public buses, relics from the Second World War, trundled through the streets, spewing out fumes. There was a dramatic absence of private cars, the common mode of transport being pick-up trucks also left behind from the war. Devoid of restaurants or cafes, Rangoon felt lacklustre and dispirited where the only thing flourishing was the black market. The crowded Scotts Market provided a striking contrast to the outside gloom, with its colourful stalls bursting with clothes, jewellery, shoes and electronics, all smuggled across the border from neighbouring Thailand. The market hustled and bustled with enterprise and locals haggling over prices. My sister and I would trail behind my mother as she went from stall to stall and all of us would come home elated from our outing.

On Sunday evenings the four of us would go to the bund along Inya Lake and gaze despondently at the water, wondering whether we would ever be able to leave this place. Because there was little contact with the outside world, it was easy to feel forgotten. Even my father said it wouldn't take much for the Ministry to forget his (and our) existence. My favourite was the Shwedagon Pagoda, towering over the city in its golden splendour. It shone like a beacon of hope through the smokiness, illuminating the city with its majestic poise.

One day my mother noticed that my sister was hobbling around the house.

"What's happened to your foot?" she asked.

"It's hurting," said my sister, and lifted the sole of her foot where a giant corn had erupted.

"Oh my goodness, it's a monster," I cried out.

"It looks infected," my mother said after surveying my sister's foot carefully. "It has pus in it. I'll have to take you to the doctor."

My sister and I looked at each other in alarm. 'Doctor' was a dreaded word in Rangoon back then because of the poor medical conditions, and all of us prayed no one would get sick and ever have to visit the hospital. Now it appeared that there was no recourse but to take Aparna to the doctor.

The following day, the three of us found ourselves in a clinic that had been recommended to my mother by a local friend. It was an old, dilapidated building that looked like a makeshift clinic, with bare shelves and no signs of medical staff. Medicines were in short supply in those days, as were doctors, since many of them had left the country over the years, never to return.

There were several people waiting to see the doctor who was on his way, we were told. Finally, the doctor arrived and it was our turn. He examined my sister's foot and told my mother, "We will have to remove this immediately." The attending nurse produced a small pump and sprayed my sister's foot generously with what was presumably an anaesthetic. A few minutes later, the nurse took out a pair of scissors and lopped off the corn while my sister shrieked in pain.

"I can't believe they actually did that!" Aparna would shudder everytime she recalled the 'corn episode'. "I was in agony, I thought I was going to die!"

"I swear, it felt like a scene from a horror movie," I said. "It all happened so quickly! Can you believe they didn't have local anaesthetic in that clinic, only that spray! No wonder Mom nearly fainted. Can't believe you actually survived that!"

---

The Indian flag fluttered in a gentle morning breeze. It was Independence Day and the embassy staff had congregated on the freshly manicured lawns of the Ambassador's residence for the flag hoisting ceremony. All our lives, in each and every foreign posting, flag hoisting had always been a special moment. The Ambassador's residence in Rangoon was an old colonial-style bungalow with a wide lawn and a tennis court. The flag unfurled and we all sang the national anthem, as rose petals gently showered down upon us.

My sister and I stood beside our mother, watching my father approach the podium. The Ambassador was away, and my father was stepping in to read the Prime Minister's address. He faced the small gathering. I marvelled at how calm and composed he always was. A natural orator, stage fright and nerves were emotions he rarely experienced. After he had read out the official speech, he spoke to all of us about our responsibilities in a foreign land, about being far away from home, about holding our banner high, always.

It didn't matter which country we were in. On Independence Day, we all came together, under the embrace of the flag, no matter how foreign the ground underneath our feet and the sky above.

---

My father obtained a travel permit to visit cities outside Rangoon for his work. This special permission granted by the Foreign Office included his family, and thus allowed us to see other parts of the country tightly sealed off to foreigners. That was how we went to Mandalay, where we saw the room in which the great Indian freedom fighter Bal Gangadhar Tilak had been imprisoned for six years by the British. In the isolation of his prison, Tilak had the tenacity to write *Gita Rahasya*, a treatise on the *Bhagvad Gita*. For my father, a devout student of history, going to Mandalay was a pilgrimage; he had received special approval to see Tilak's room.

Burma was as beautiful as a ruby, glowing with ancient temples and fertile fields. A local Burmese gentleman took us on a cruise along the Irrawaddy Delta, where we slept on the boat for three nights as it sailed past mangroves, wetlands, huts and pagodas, reflecting an enchanted land waiting to be awakened.

The Indo-Burma border was strictly off limits, even to Indian embassy officials. Professionally, it was important for Indian diplomats to visit the border checkpoints since it was the route that connected Burma to northeast India. In the late nineties, India would be invited to build a road connecting the northeastern state of Manipur to the adjacent territories in today's Myanmar. But back then, despite numerous requests made to the Burmese authorities, permission to visit those areas was not granted. In central Burma, there continued to be settlements of Indians, many of them from Uttar Pradesh, Bihar and Orissa, who had migrated as farm labour during the colonial period when the British governed Burma out of Calcutta. When the Japanese attacked Burma in 1942, a large number of these Indians fled on foot, through the mountainous, forested border of northern Burma into India. While many perished along the way, others got left behind. It was this ethnic group which constituted one of the most impoverished communities in Burma during our time. When my father visited these clusters, we too went along with him on long road trips through the interiors of Burma, where community leaders in small towns like Zeyawaddy and Chautaga welcomed us with sweets and flowers. They spoke Bihari dialects and were connected to an India of a bygone era. They yearned for India to which they desperately sought to return. Discriminated by the majority and displaced from their homeland, these people of Indian origin were stateless, had no passports and could barely make ends meet. Their pitiful plight was a source of deep frustration for my father, who knew the Government of India could do nothing to help them. Besides, my father was acutely aware that while he was meeting with local Indians, the Burmese military and intelligentsia were on the prowl, watching him closely, suspicious that the Indian government could stir up trouble by instigating the local leaders.

---

By learning mahjong, my mother befriended a few Burmese families who had special permits to interact with foreigners. She found them warm and hospitable. Sometimes my mother would have an outdoor party and her Burmese guests would delight in the durian tree in our garden, a fruit that was much sought after by the locals. The guests would look up at the ripened fruit, hoping to be the lucky recipients in case one or two durians were to fall.

In the repressive atmosphere of Rangoon, my mother remained the pivot around which our household turned, the one who could burnish our bleak environs with her creativity. She organised picnics for us and wrote plays for the embassy children to keep us entertained. One play required all of us to be insects.

"I've written a play in which you will be a butterfly, Ashwini, and Aparna, you will be the lizard. Rohan and Raj will be the beetles," she said, referring to our neighbour's two boys.

"I don't think they will like that too much," I said.

My sister, very proud of her role, decided to immerse herself into her character, which she did by strutting around the house wearing a cut-out of a lizard we'd made with cardboard, all the while practising reptilian sounds that made me recoil. Despite its entomological theme, the play generated a high degree of excitement among the children in the compound. My mother aptly titled the play, "The Buddies of Budd Road."

While I preferred to hole up in my room and listen to music, Aparna was a busybody who liked traipsing around the garden, or disappearing to the neighbours' houses. When she wasn't climbing trees, she would start climbing on tables and cupboards in the house to see how far she could jump, much to my mother's chagrin. A tomboy who aligned herself with the character George from Enid Blyton's *Famous Five* series, Aparna was most offended that Rohan and Raj, who lived in the adjacent compound, did not want to play with her. They found her annoying and devised ingenuous ways to hide from her. One evening she returned from their house, disappointed that she hadn't found them. It was getting dark. The path that led from their cottage to ours was narrow and lined with thick bushes. She suddenly heard a rustle in one of the bushes and saw something glistening a few feet ahead of her. She walked curiously in the direction of the glow, and as she stepped forward, she quickly realised that the amber reflection was coming off a python's skin – mottled orange and gold, no more than a foot away from her. She stood there, frozen.

"The snake and I looked at each other," she told us later, when she came screaming into the house. A storyteller with a great flair for drama, Aparna gave us a passionate account of her Encounter with the Python.

"My goodness, that is so scary!" cried my mother. "You should not be walking that way in the dark! Who told you to go to Rohan's house at this hour?"

"The snake was on the main path! It was so long and its eyes were shining, I didn't know which way to run. Finally it slithered away."

Snakes and scorpions were a daily hazard in Rangoon that required us to be constantly alert. Legends and folklore abounded and we were told that if you killed a snake, its relatives would come find you. It was a disconcerting thought.

Every night, just before falling asleep, my sister and I would hear the cry of the gecko, echoing through the quietness of the night. *Tawk-te, tawk-te.* Both of us would count along with the gecko and if it called out seven times, we would look at each other triumphantly because the seventh cry was considered lucky.

When I turned fourteen, the question of my schooling could no longer be ignored.

"You will have to go to a proper school," said my father. Since we could not afford the international school, after much discussion, it was decided that I would go to our hometown Pune in India where I would live with my paternal grandmother and my newly married uncle and aunt. My heart sank.

"You will leave us?" said my sister, eyes big in her thin face.

My sister would tell me, years later, that after I left, she was so lonely she took to tree climbing with a vengeance. She climbed every tree in the garden, along with a cat, which she had adopted.

My parents didn't have the heart to say no to her exploits.

---

The horizon was dotted with pagodas. Three thousand of them lined the skyline of the ancient city of Bagan.

"Let's count them," Aparna suggested. We began, but we could only reach fifty. By then, the stupas became a blur in the dusky sky. Staring at the stupas scattered across the arid land was a haunting reminder that my time to leave was imminent. Our family trip to Bagan was the epilogue to my short chapter in Burma.

A new adventure was about to begin.

*The author at Fergusson College in Pune, 1985*

# Feels Like Home

## INDIA
*1981–1985*

## Pune

1981 was the year of the epic battle between two Bollywood blockbusters, *Rocky* and *Love Story*. Girls were split into the Sanjay Dutt or Kumar Gaurav camps and never could the twain meet. Helmed by these two freshly minted twenty-something actors, both films were triggering mass hysteria around the country: Sanjay Dutt with his bad-boy image had girls slitting their wrists, while others were swooning over chocolate hero Kumar Gaurav. I trooped to the cinema along with my cousins, joining them excitedly in the whistling and clapping that ensued when the heroes made their first appearance on screen. Like everyone, I too was swept off my feet by the euphoria these films were evoking. After watching the films twice, I cast my vote for Sanjay Dutt, whose ruggedness, in my view, overpowered Kumar Gaurav's boyish innocence. I found myself humming the mega-hit songs that blared from every shop and street corner, and gazing up star-struck at the life-size posters of the two actors that loomed large over various parts of the city. One simply could not escape the fervour. The seductive and all-encompassing effect of Hindi films on the Indian psyche was evident everywhere. Bollywood was a central theatre where emotions of an entire nation seemed to play out. After the despondency of Rangoon, the crowds and energy in Pune were delightfully stimulating.

Joining a new school in ninth grade, in a country famed for its notoriously high academic standards, was not something I would have voluntarily inflicted on myself at the age of fifteen. Sometimes I wished I'd gone to boarding school like many other children from the Foreign Service; at least that would have prepared me for the brutal rigour of Indian schools. But as my mother would often tell me, "Your father and I never dreamed of sending you away, we wanted you to be with us." That's how I tagged along with them from country to country, and ended up in my paternal grandmother's house in the outskirts of Pune during my formative high school years.

After the small, friendly school in Rangoon, the all-girls St. Joseph's Convent felt impersonal and intimidating. Girls of all shapes and sizes milled around in a sea of unfamiliarity, in their beige uniforms, red belts, white socks and black shoes. With my two plaits, which my grandmother neatly oiled and braided every morning, I should ostensibly have blended right in, but there was something about me that spelt 'foreigner' in big and bold letters. That I didn't know a single person in the school did not make settling in easier. The first week, I found myself struggling to understand the equations the chemistry teacher was writing on the board. All around me, girls were hastily scribbling notes as they tried to keep up with Ms Naik's swift pace. Like most Indians, she talked very fast.

"Who got 2 out of 10? Whose paper is this?" Ms Naik waved a sheet in the air. When no hands were raised, I realised in horror that the paper was *mine*. Forty-five pairs of eyes turned to stare at me.

"This is a *Fail*," declared Ms Naik, showing no mercy, as she dropped the test paper on my desk. My desperate desire to hide felt like a migraine, my constant companion. Here I was, in my own country, with nowhere to run.

Burma felt very far away.

---

"We called you the Girl from Burma," laughed Reena and Mansi, the two popular back-benchers in my class who wore imported clothes, chewed gum and biked to school. I felt gawky and gauche around them, with my oiled hair and wrap-around skirts from Rangoon's Scotts Market.

"You were rather too friendly for a new girl," they would tell me years later.

I didn't want to confide in them that it was an *act*, a performance I had polished over the years, having been the 'new girl' so many times in my life. Like almost everyone else in our school, Reena and Mansi had grown up in Pune and spent their entire lives in St Joseph's, which was their second home. They knew every corner and every corridor of the building, every teacher and even the girls in the grades above and below us. I was envious that Mansi and Reena had grown up together, and would take their friendship with them into the future, while I perfected the art of bidding farewell every three years.

"*O Sajna*," mimicked Reena and all the girls laughed. My face turned red. I had sung the song at a school function recently; for a new girl to volunteer to sing was seen as rather audacious and caused a fair deal of tittering in class. Embarrassed, I did not offer to sing again, but a few weeks later, I was pleasantly surprised when some of my classmates suggested my name for an upcoming school programme. From then on, I sang regularly. Singing Hindi film songs became an outlet that tooled me to cope with my new environment. For the first time in my adolescent life, I was beginning to feel a sense of belonging, the foreign-ness starting to diminish. I had been a chameleon in search of my natural habitat for too long; it was a relief, at last, to find that the flora and fauna around me was *native*, not borrowed.

It took me a year to figure out the Indian curriculum, but once I mastered the art of cramming, it worked like magic. I memorised every single paragraph on every single page. I could recite my history book upside down; I even knew where the commas were. With Ms Naik's voice ringing in my ears *This is a Fail! This is a Fail!,* I too went for tuition in the evenings like all the other girls to conquer my fear of science and math. Hindi, a subject I could barely read or write, became my nemesis, along with civics, which my uncle would patiently try to explain to me every evening after he returned from work. I found cramming for nine subjects far less torturous than having to share the single squatting toilet in my grandmother's house with four others.

---

The upside of returning to India was it brought me into my grandmother's embrace. A petite, determined woman, my grandmother lived with her younger son and his wife who was a just few years older than me, and with whom I instantly hit it off. People flocked to my grandmother's small home at all times of the day, drawn to her warmth and hospitality. My grandmother's younger sister who had never married, and whom I also called 'grandmother', lived with us and together, they showered me with much love and attention, feeling sorry for my 'orphaned' state. The hustle and bustle of the crowded household helped thwart the bouts of homesickness that threatened to engulf me every now and again, especially as I didn't get to see my parents and sister for two years because we couldn't afford the travel.

My *atya* (aunt) Sudha, who lived in the more affluent part of town, would whisk me off to her house on weekends and treat me to pizza and fresh alphonso mango ice cream that she made at home. For the first time, I experienced community living, where no boundaries existed, where neighbours became part of extended households, and everyone was welcome to stay as long as they wished and drink as many cups of tea as they liked.

I shared a bed with my grandmothers, which was just big enough to accommodate the three of us. At bedtime, we would tuck in the mosquito net, chat in sleepy voices, and fall asleep, one by one, with junior grandmother snoring loudly in the middle. When my alarm went off at 3am, my preferred time to study, it was junior grandma who would wake up with a start, and gently nudge me awake. She would move my legs to the side, raise the mosquito net cautiously, and clamber down from the bed. Her soft footsteps padded across the small room, while I sat up in bed, rubbing my eyes, wishing I could turn over and snuggle back to sleep. Because she knew I was terrified of lizards, junior grandma would switch on the dim light above the desk and do a thorough check for the large beady-eyed creatures that prowled around at night, sometimes on the floor, holding giant cockroaches in their mouths. She would then motion to me that the path was clear, and I would climb out of the mosquito net and settle at the desk, while she quietly returned to bed, next to her sleeping sister. That was how we slept, huddled together, for the next two years, my grandmothers' spectacles and dentures all neatly lined up by their bedside, and their slippers on the floor, perfectly positioned in pairs. Looking at their slender frames covered in saris that they themselves had stitched into blankets instilled in me a fierce protectiveness towards my petite grandmothers and a desire to hold on to them forever.

---

Two years later, my father was transferred to Delhi and once again, our family was reunited. After small-town Pune, the capital felt frighteningly unfamiliar, the big bad city that sprawled out in unknown directions, with the staring eyes of men that seemed to follow me everywhere I went. Delhi felt like a jungle in which predators looked for targets to 'eve-tease', an all-too familiar word in every Indian girl's lexicon. Aparna and I were completely unprepared for the streets of Delhi, which felt mean and merciless. I became terrified of walking out of our home after a boy flashed me. He did it again the next day and the next. I remained at home for three days till the boy went away. One afternoon, my sister and I were walking to the market down the road when a man on a scooter slowed down beside me, touched my breasts and drove off, leaving me humiliated and enraged, eyes smarting with furious tears. Learning to ignore the stares of lecherous men was an exercise that required a composure and stoicism I didn't possess at sixteen. I refused to go to the market again, much to my mother's exasperation. It made me upset that my mother would not notice the louts; instead she would become impatient and scold me, "Do you really think they don't have anything better to do than to stare at you?"

While Aparna was only ten, the age difference between us seemed to have vanished in tandem with her rising maturity. She was all grown up, using big words when she spoke, reading books that I was not even aware existed on my father's bookshelf. We became inseparable. We'd listen to music on our cassette player, and Michael Jackson's *Billie Jean* would bounce off the rickety glass windows of our verandah. I'd play the song over and over, neither of us wanting it to end. The energy lifted us, swept us off our feet, leaving us inexplicably breathless. Michael Jackson's *Thriller* was electrifying the world.

My father, meanwhile, walked around with a bounce in his step. He had virtually vanished off the radar the two years that he had been in Burma, and returning to headquarters, to work at the Ministry of External Affairs in South Block, gave him a heady sense of belonging and relevance.

The year my father arrived in Delhi, 1983, coincided with India winning the World Cup. If there was one thing my father had missed dearly in his postings abroad, it was watching cricket. To be in Delhi the same year that India won the World Cup made him simply delirious with happiness.

---

As if the streets of Delhi weren't bad enough, the beast of school admissions proved just as unnerving. For Foreign Service families returning to headquarters, it was an admissions nightmare, since securing a spot in one of the coveted schools depended purely on 'connections,' or *jugaad*, a practice my parents, after years of living abroad, were not conversant with. Aparna sat at home for four months, while my mother complained bitterly to my father about our lack of 'influence'. When the summer ended and brought in the rains, Aparna was still sitting at home. She missed Rangoon dreadfully: her cosy school, the pomelo tree in the garden and all the cats she had adopted. Delhi felt aloof and unwelcoming, a city where no school was willing to take her in. She walked around the house despondently, wondering aloud if we were being punished by the jealous-types for having lived abroad for so many years.

A chance meeting between my father and an Air Force officer at a dinner party proved fortuitous. When the officer heard of my sister's plight, he exclaimed, "Doesn't the Foreign Service help its children with school admissions?" He took it upon himself to resolve the matter, and his intervention helped my sister get admission to the Air Force School. As for me, I landed a spot at the very posh Modern School in Vasant Vihar thanks to a casual conversation between my father and his senior colleague during a round of golf.

A cluster of charming brick buildings with gentle alcoves, set against an expanse of green, was the setting for the exclusive Modern School nestled in one of Delhi's most affluent neighbourhoods. The amber bricks provided nurturing warmth, especially on winter days. Boys and girls in sky blue uniforms floated around. Modern was a fashionable school with its fair share of fashionable people, Delhi's rich elite that lived in upscale neighbourhoods like Panchsheel, Saket and Defence Colony. Plenty of industrialists' kids drove flashy cars and threw lavish parties. Suddenly I was arguing with my parents for permission to go to these parties and over curfew times.

The first few months in school were marked with great anticipation, romantic idealism and a series of schoolgirl crushes. When a good-looking boy with tousled hair asked me out, I instantly said yes and proceeded to fall madly in love, having never experienced the rush of teenage romance. The novelty of the infatuation was far more seductive than the boy himself. Three months later when he broke up with me, I was more devastated at the idea of 'being dumped' than the realisation that we had very little in common to begin with. For the first few days, I walked around utterly crestfallen until I was struck with the epiphany that in fact I did not miss him as much as I had expected to.

Over time I found myself drawn to like-minded people who helped me overcome my very first heartbreak. We would hang out at Priya Cinema after school, eat butterscotch ice cream at Nirula's or meet at each other's homes. We were a bunch of teenagers with wistful dreams and wishful thinking, as we journeyed through these impressionable years together. When I sang *Ajeeb Dastan Hai Yeh* at the farewell party for our seniors, I felt the applause from my friends echoing in my head long afterwards.

Years later they would tell me how they would be reminded of this evening whenever they heard *Ajeeb Dastan* on the radio. Two years later we would go our separate ways, carrying with us snapshots of an idyllic school life, framed by sunshine filtering through brick arches.

—❈—

The last day at Modern School arrived sooner than anyone of us would have wished. The buoyant mood was tinged with sentimentality, a parting of ways imminent. Two years cocooned in a space that was safe and protected from the vagaries of the outside world; college loomed on the horizon, the great big unknown.

Two years, three years, two years, three years, that's how my life had been so far, and as I grew older, the associations had started to become more meaningful and impactful. The feeling of belonging had deepened over the last two years, as an appreciation for my own culture and identity took root. Psychological and physical changes shape adolescence, as they did mine, a journey of self-discovery, upheaval and turbulence, marked by frequent changes and disruptions.

These and many thoughts surged through my mind as we milled about in school, saying our goodbyes. Following tradition, everyone scribbled messages on each other's uniforms till there was not an inch of space left on anyone's clothing. In the past few weeks, I'd begun to spend time with a boy whom I had grown fond of, even though I didn't fully reciprocate his romantic feelings towards me.

Rishab was sporty, quirky and always respectful; I appreciated the courtesy with which he treated me. Unlike some of the other industrialists' sons, he wasn't flashy or flamboyant. As he walked up towards me, I greeted him with a warm smile. I knew I'd probably never see him again. We began to talk about the upcoming summer holidays and where we were headed.

"Want to go for a drive? I'll drop you home later," he said.

My first instinct was to say no, but I found myself saying

yes. Soon I was sitting behind him on his scooter and we were driving about the streets of Delhi. It was the middle of the afternoon and the sun was blazing directly above our heads.

"Should we go to this park? It's so hot, maybe we can get an ice cream," Rishab said.

We drove into a garden. He parked his scooter and we walked inside. It felt nice and cool under the shade, after the blistering heat. There was a small slope in front of us, and at the top stood a monument, a miniature version of some of the more majestic tombs that adorned the famous parks in Delhi. Rishab suggested a walk up the slope to get a better view.

"How was your exam yesterday?" I asked him, as we climbed up the small hill and found a shady spot alongside the wall of the monument.

"Eco was tougher than I'd expected. Don't think I'll get the marks for SRCC."

"And me for Stephen's," I said.

Suddenly, we heard voices; they seemed to be coming up the hill. Six men came into view. They saw us sitting by the wall and called out to one another. To our dismay, they began walking towards us. One of them sneered. "Doing *masti* when you should be in school?"

Another one said, "Let's teach them a lesson!" They all laughed. My heart was thumping so loudly, I was sure they could hear it. "We have to run," Rishab said to me, in an undertone. But there was no place to run. The men surrounded us, their faces dark and mocking. My skirt suddenly felt very short, my knees exposed. Our clothes, covered in squiggles and shapes and "Don't forget me!", "Love ya forever" felt horribly conspicuous.

"What's all this on your clothes?" one of the men came up to me, bloodshot eyes travelling up and down my body. I started to shiver. Rishab was telling the men we were returning to school and if we didn't get back, the principal would report us missing. He motioned me to follow him and we tried to cut through the men, hoping desperately they would make way for us.

A small crowd of onlookers had gathered, observing us from a safe distance; but they looked nervous, not wanting to intervene. One of the men grabbed Rishab and shoved him towards the back of the tomb. Both disappeared from view. Two of the men ordered me down the slope, to where their jeep was parked. I felt someone pushing me into the back of the jeep.

"Get out of the jeep!" screamed Rishab, his face convulsed with fear, as he came running down the slope towards us. He talked rapidly with the men and I would realise later he was negotiating with them for my release. My legs trembled violently, yet in that split second, I managed to clamber out of the jeep and ran as fast as I could, out of the park, onto the street, headlong into oncoming traffic. A cacophony of honking and harsh sunlight blinded me, as I continued to run. Would Rishab follow me or would they hurt him, now that I had escaped?

I didn't know whether to keep on running or to wait for him, when he appeared next to me on his scooter and drove us at breakneck speed till my house came into view. That's when we both started crying.

I did not leave the confines of my home for several days nor did I tell my parents about the incident. I couldn't rid myself of the men's faces, which continued to choke me with terror. I would replay the chain of events over and over in my head. Surely it was a divine, inexplicable force that had given me the courage to jump out. Racked by fits of uncontrollable shuddering, I was forever haunted by what could have happened had they driven off with me in the back of the jeep.

The incident marked a natural culmination to my short-lived friendship with Rishab, but the incident scarred my consciousness for years to come.

---

Dark clouds were gathering across India's political horizon when my father assumed his role as Joint Secretary at the Ministry of External Affairs. He was assigned to the critically important BSM desk, dealing with neighbouring countries Bangladesh, Sri Lanka, Myanmar and the Maldives, all of which required sensitive handling. That he had to report directly to the Foreign Secretary and Foreign Minister Narasimha Rao added to the pressure.

"Developments in Sri Lanka had to be closely followed not only for the sake of bilateral relations, but also because of internal repercussions within India, in Tamil Nadu," recalled my father.

The crisis in Sri Lanka blew up in the summer of 1983. An attack by Tamil guerrillas in which thirteen soldiers were killed, sparked anti-Tamil riots around Sri Lanka in which hundreds died. It would be the beginning of a nearly two-decade-long war between the government of Sri Lanka and the Liberation Tigers of Tamil Eelam or LTTE, a guerrilla organisation that was fighting for a separate Tamil state in the northern and eastern parts of the island. The Sri Lankan government, always suspicious of Indian involvement in its Tamil terror problem, was convinced of 'the Indian hand' in the latest attacks.

"After the '83 crisis, we proposed a devolution package, but the Sri Lankan government rejected it," said my father. "The situation was becoming extremely serious. It was inevitable, Mrs Gandhi was pulled deeper into the quagmire of Sri Lankan and Tamil politics." These developments put Sri Lanka at the heart of India's foreign policy, with extensive debates in parliament where impassioned Members of Parliament from Tamil Nadu would speak on the conflict.

"All this while, the Tamil terror groups were becoming stronger," recalled my father. "The LTTE under Prabhakaran would emerge as the most feared and deadly terror group in the region." Four years later, in a controversial move, India would send in the IPKF (Indian Peacekeeping Force) to Sri Lanka, a bold initiative by young Prime Minister Rajiv Gandhi that would end in a military disaster in which over a thousand Indian soldiers perished.

Little did Rajiv Gandhi foresee this decision would mark the beginning of the end, and sound a tocsin for the minatory events that lay ahead. In May 1991, Rajiv Gandhi would be killed by the LTTE in a horrific attack that numbed the nation. He was then only forty-seven years old.

It was the beginning of a summer pock-marked by nightmares. My own nightmares merged into a larger, shadowy sky, as the summer turned sinister and ominous clouds settled over the nation.

Prime Minister Indira Gandhi's decision to storm the Golden Temple in Amritsar, the religious centre for Sikhs, put the nation on edge. Sikh radicals, who had made the Golden Temple their base, were demanding a separate homeland and their call for secession was intensifying with each passing day. When negotiations collapsed, the Indian Government took the decision to send in the army to flush out the militants, a move that sent nervous ripples across the capital. For the next six days, the Indian Army battled it out with the Sikh militants in what came to be known as Operation Blue Star. It would end in victory for the Indian Government, but turn out to be a poisoned chalice for the Prime Minister a few months later.

October 31, 1984, started as a normal working day. It was 9.30am as my father headed out of Chanakyapuri towards South Block. As he came to Race Course Road, several police officers stopped him and motioned him to turn back. When my father reached South Block via an alternative route, there was pandemonium in the Ministry. He was told that Prime Minister Indira Gandhi had been assassinated, but no one was allowed to confirm the news. So much so that my father did not even tell my mother and me while we were returning home from the market in a three-wheeler, laden with bags of fresh vegetables and fruits.

We sensed something was amiss when the driver told us he had heard something 'terrible' had happened to the Prime

Minister. As soon as we were home, we switched on the television and radio, but both Doordarshan and All India Radio were maintaining an eerie silence; all the while rumours swirled furiously around the country.

It was only later that afternoon that the news was formally announced to the nation. The Prime Minister of India was dead, killed in an act of revenge for Operation Blue Star, which she had launched four months earlier to flush out Sikh radicals from the Golden Temple. One of her own security guards, a Sikh, had gunned Mrs Gandhi down, as she walked from her residence to her office located within the grounds of her home.

She died instantly.

For the next several days, plumes of smoke darkened the skyline as Delhi burned. Anti-Sikh riots engulfed the city as frenzied mobs attacked Sikh establishments, dragging Sikh men and women out of their homes, shops, trains and buses with a chilling vengeance. While the official death count of the numbers of Sikhs massacred was 3,000, the unofficial number was as high as 7,000. We were in the midst of the worst sectarian violence that would sear the nation's conscience for years to come. As we sat holed up inside our home, the nation continued to erupt, with each day bringing fresh reports of carnage and destruction.

Aparna and I sat in our room horrified by what we were hearing. We heard horror stories of Sikhs being set aflame and clubbed to death, their businesses burned to the ground, women raped, and hooligans roaming the streets with weapons.

Then one evening there was panic in our colony, with rumours that rioters were approaching our neighbourhood. "The mobs are coming! The mobs are coming!" some people were shouting, and we sat terrified inside our homes, with the lights shut and the curtains drawn.

The blood that flowed into the streets during the anti-Sikh riots was a shocking reminder of how vulnerable race relations were in this country, how the fault lines were constantly threatening to rip the nation apart.

It was the middle of the night when my father silently opened the door and four figures filed in, huddled in dark clothes, eyes filled with terror. They were our closest friends, the Singh family, and they asked if they could spend the night in our home. They were Sikhs, but they were our friends first, and my father said they could stay with us for as long as they wished and until they could return safely to their home.

Our household help was visibly distressed and angry when he saw the Sikh family in our home the next morning. He told my father he was putting all our lives at risk. Sulky and angry, he didn't speak to my father for several days afterwards.

India now had a new head of government. At forty, Rajiv Gandhi became India's youngest Prime Minister. He was the reluctant leader, thrust into the spotlight, trying to restore calm and peace in the nation, even as he grappled with the overwhelming grief of losing his own mother.

Operation Blue Star, Gandhi's assassination and the Bhopal tragedy, India's calamitous industrial disaster, made it a year of anarchy for the country.

I left India after five years, the longest I had lived anywhere thus far. The continuity had provided me with stability through my teens, a welcome relief to the constant swings that had been my life so far. Being on home ground laid a foundation for a relationship with my country that would become intimate, emotional and lifelong. It would also be the last time I would spend an extended period of time in India.

Author singing at the KBS song contest for foreigners, 1986

*The Land of the Morning Calm*

## SOUTH KOREA
*1986–1989*

# Seoul

Silence permeated the woods. I felt a rush of autumn cool against my cheeks. Around us, a phalanx of pines soared into the sky, a deep green piercing the ridges around us. Shinjin climbed briskly, notwithstanding the robes swathing her, while I struggled to keep pace. Every now and then we would catch a glimpse of rock beyond the trees, a reminder of how mountainous this land was.

Shinjin stopped a few feet ahead, and turned around to look at me. "I'm famished, aren't you?"

"I was wondering when you were going to say that," I panted.

"You do know me quite well!" Shinjin laughed. "Don't worry, we're nearly there, another ten minutes."

We made strange bedfellows, Shinjin and I, as we trekked up a rough path that cut through granite, the native geological stone formations surrounding us. I'd met Shinjin, a British Buddhist monk, at a cultural event a few weeks back. With her clean-shaven head, sparkling eyes and hearty laugh, she stuck out in the sea of Korean uniformity. A fascination with Buddhism had brought her to South Korea some ten years ago, and upon arriving here, Shinjin had immersed herself into the teachings and practices of Zen Buddhism, which routinely led to her disappearing into the mountains for months on end to meditate. Shinjin's fondness for Indian food made her a regular visitor to our house. In between bites of dal and *paneer*, she would share with us her philosophy and outlook on Buddhism. Fascinated by her accounts of travel through South Korea, I asked her if she could take me along to visit a monastery. That was how we found ourselves in this craggy Korean mountainside in the outskirts of Seoul.

We walked up a steep, narrow path and suddenly came to a clearing. A few feet away from us stood a small Buddhist temple, its grey-red roofs pointing outwards like two arms raised in worship towards the sky. Shinjin was quiet for a few minutes. Finally, she said, "This is the place I wanted to take you to."

The temple stood on a slight elevation, with steps leading up to its entrance. We removed our shoes and walked inside, into a warm, incense-filled sanctum, where a large statue of Buddha stood on a wooden platform. The interior of the monastery was as austere as the external façade, designed to blend with the natural rocky surroundings. Two monks, dressed like Shinjin, came up to us and greeted us warmly.

"This is my Indian friend," Shinjin introduced us in Korean and we all bowed deeply. Shinjin spoke to them for a few minutes after which the monks led us past a square courtyard to the main shrine of worship. An open pavilion provided a serene view of the mountains surrounding the temple, beyond that were the meditation spaces and residential quarters. The monks motioned us to take our seats next to them on bamboo mats, and offered me incense sticks to stick into an ash-filled urn. Then, along with Shinjin, they began chanting.

Sitting next to Shinjin, listening to their prayers and the soothing cadence of their voices, I was filled with immense relief. My decision had been impulsive, but at that very moment, as I chanted the mantras, I knew it couldn't have been a better one.

Just a few months ago, I had been sitting in a dingy dorm room at Fergusson College in Pune, sharing a dirty loo with a dozen girls. The flush had not been working for two days and sanitary pads were piling up in the corner of the toilet. The stench was beginning to spread down the corridor, and since my room was the closest to the loo, I got the full onslaught. My roommate, a good-natured soul, lit incense sticks in our room to diffuse the stink. While it was a genius idea, it only mildly prevented both of us from suffocating.

My parents and sister were in South Korea, while I joined Fergusson College, my parents' alma mater. My freshman year was not going according to plan. It might have been the annual college festival in which I got a chance to sing a popular Bollywood film song that keeled me over. On the evening of the programme, large crowds of students began to pour into the big hall, ready to have a good time, since exams had just finished. As I stepped in front of the mike, overlooking the packed hall, I had the worst attack of stage fright in my seventeen-year-old history. It felt like the entire population of Fergusson College was crammed into this space, waiting to hear me perform. My throat clamped up and my legs began to tremble.

"Mera gaam kaatha parey, jahan doodh ki nadiya bhaye." The shaky, quivery voice didn't sound anything like my own. "*Jahan Koyal toh koh gaye.*"

And then my brain slipped into abeyance. The lyrics of the next line eluded me, as did the melody. I couldn't rely on muscle memory either, because unlike many of the old Lata Mangeshkar tunes I'd been singing since childhood, this was a song I had only recently learnt. When the organisers saw that I was frozen on stage, one of them ran up to me to escort me off stage and spare me from what was about to happen. To my horror, a few tomatoes landed on stage, accompanied by loud whistles and laughter, which seemed to follow us all the way to outside the building. The only silver lining to my swansong was that it occurred at the end of freshman year and the college emptied out the next day, which saved me from the humiliation of earning the sobriquet of 'the girl who screwed up on stage'.

It became amply clear that my days at Fergusson College were numbered.

---

When it was time to visit my parents and sister over the summer holidays, I carefully packed all my belongings, leaving no trace of my existence in the dorm room. My goodbye to my roommate had a deep tinge of finality. On the flight to Seoul, I devised various strategies on how I would break the news to my parents. I found the opportunity a few days after my arrival, over breakfast.

"I'm not going back," I told my parents, casually buttering my toast. There was a stunned silence at the breakfast table.

"Not going back?" repeated my father. "What do you mean?"

Aparna suppressed a giggle. She was the only one privy to the information I was about to reveal.

"I'm not going back to Pune."

Since no one spoke, I continued speaking. "I'm staying here in Seoul."

Finally, my mother spoke. "But what about college? You've only just finished your first year."

"Has something happened?" asked my father, looking concerned.

"Nothing's happened. It's just that I'm really homesick. I just want to be here with all of you."

Aparna had a big smile. Her eyes danced with happiness. "You don't have to go back," she said cheerfully.

My parents stared at me in silence.

"No one will miss me there," I said. "Half the professors don't even show up for lectures. No one cares if you go to class or not."

"How can you say that about colleges in Pune," said my mother looking affronted. "That too about Fergusson College!" My mother's father had been a professor of Political Science at Fergusson, and to my mother, the college was a sanctum of higher education where freedom fighters had studied in the past. Both my parents were products of Pune's venerated educational system, which they continued to hold in the highest regard. They took any criticism of Pune colleges very personally.

"Fergusson College is one of the finest institutions," said my father, looking at me in disbelief.

"It's not what it was in your days, Dad," I finished buttering my toast. "Anyway," I looked at my father, "you will have to find me a college here or I'll take a gap year. Because I'm *not* going back."

"How am I going to produce a college for you here?" asked my father. There was a long silence, as my parents looked at each other.

"But I suppose we can't force you to go back, can we?" my father's eyes twinkled, my mother looked at me and smiled, and Aparna thumped me on my back and shouted out, "Yes!"

It was good to be home again. Everything was going to be all right.

Well, almost.

---

My parents and sister had arrived in Seoul only a few months ago and were still in the throes of getting adjusted to their new surroundings. As first-time Ambassador, my father was extremely preoccupied, trying to get his head around the responsibilities of running the mission, a reasonably large embassy with several officers and local staff. Now, instead of focusing on India-Korea relations, he had a bigger crisis on hand: his elder daughter was on the verge of becoming a college dropout.

My father hastened to make enquiries. His worst fears were very quickly confirmed; none of the local universities offered undergraduate degrees in English. The medium of instruction in the colleges was Korean. Just when we were all beginning to lose hope, a door opened, by a stroke of serendipity, at an official luncheon where my mother happened to be seated next to an American woman who worked in the military. She casually mentioned to my mother that her son had got his undergraduate degree from the University of Maryland which had a small campus in Seoul. It was a eureka moment for my mother who came rushing home in a state of great excitement, shouting "Ashwini, I've found a college for you!"

My euphoria was short-lived. When I found myself standing outside Yongsan Military Base, a heavily guarded and gated complex in the heart of Seoul, I wondered whether learning

*Author wearing hanbok, a traditional Korean dress.*

Korean might not have been a better alternative. This was *not* your typical undergraduate college by a long mile. The leafy campus with charming brick buildings that I'd imagined, the archetypical liberal artsy college that I'd seen in glossy American brochures, were far removed from the reality of these grim buildings that loomed behind a barbed wire fencing, where I was about to stitch together the remaining parts of my college education.

I flashed my student pass at the security guard and timidly asked where the University of Maryland was. The guard motioned me towards a small, nondescript building, which did not have any semblance to an academic institution. As I got closer, I realised the one-storeyed building was a military barrack that had been converted into a makeshift classroom.

It was getting dark; the idea of taking evening classes was rather disconcerting. There were no signs of students in sweatshirts and backpacks – instead I saw several soldiers in camouflage uniforms walking towards the building. Some of them had 'Air Force' and 'Marine Corps' written across their jackets. I walked into the foyer of the building and saw a sign that read: Asian Studies 101 – THIS WAY. I was in the right place, and all the soldiers walking about were there for the same class as me! Some of them smiled at me politely and held the door as I walked in. I felt the familiar flutter of butterflies in my throat and my legs wobbled as I walked into the room. It was crowded; the class was clearly a popular one. I quickly sat down in the first empty chair I could spot, right beside the door, wishing I could melt away into invisibility.

A gentleman standing in front of a whiteboard nodded at me; he was the professor and among the few people in the room wearing civilian clothes like me. I felt an instant solidarity with him.

Once the class began, I started to relax and had the courage to look around. While most were military men and women, there were some civilians, including a few Asian Americans. Sitting alongside uniformed GIs was an education in itself. Here I was, fresh from India, smack in the centre of the biggest US army base in Asia, learning about Korean history from an American professor.

Over the next few weeks, I began to adjust to my new college campus. As part of a comprehensive bilateral defence alliance between the United States and South Korea, there were over 40,000 American soldiers stationed in the country. To cater to their educational requirements, the University of Maryland had opened a satellite campus on Yongsan Base, which was a miniature America nestled in the centre of Seoul. Burger King, Taco Bell and the Commissary stocked with the latest American provisions that the soldiers and their families might miss in the land of kimchi; it was Americana from the minute you entered the gate. Often a baseball game would be in progress, with crowds sitting in the bleachers cheering the players on. Other times you could smell the grilling of burgers and hot dogs as families barbecued, especially during the Fourth of July or Thanksgiving holidays. Sometimes when I walked around Yongsan, it was easy to forget that this was not America and that we were surrounded by a country which was strikingly different from the one that had been recreated inside this military facility.

Americans, as I discovered, were a friendly bunch of people and easy to get along with. Classes were animated, especially the one on international relations and US foreign policy. I was lucky to have Larry Burns as my professor. Pony-tailed and provocative, Larry was a visiting professor from Oregon, with a liberal flair for attacking all aspects of US foreign policy. His class was a testament to the fundamental strength of the American education system – that despite the military composition of the classroom, Professor Burns did not feel compelled to alter his leftist philosophy.

My life in Seoul was neatly compartmentalised into two; on one hand there was South Korea, a country in a tearing rush towards modernisation, and on the other, there was America, which I was vicariously living in. The Koreans, while more reserved than the Americans, were largely affable, hospitable and friendly. They called us "Indo" and said we were *ippo* (pretty). That boosted our egos.

Every now and again we would hear about student demonstrations near Yongsan Base protesting the presence of US troops in Korea. It made me aware that anti-Americanism was not new in South Korea, something I tried to push to the back of my mind as I walked around the military complex. It was also a startling reminder of how insulated we were, sitting inside the base, from the political developments that were unfolding across South Korea.

We were together again, the four of us, united in a foreign country. But this time, unlike in the past, my sister and I rarely saw our parents. They were sucked into a whirlwind of official responsibilities that began soon after arriving in Seoul. My father was so preoccupied with his new job, he seemed oblivious to our existence. Aparna would refer to him as the 'Space Cadet'. My mother too was equally distracted; her biggest worry was to secure Indian provisions, which were not available in Seoul back then. We had to rely on shipments of *ata* and lentils from Malaysia, which would arrive every few months. Because my mother was consumed by the economic and logistical management of the household while balancing the role of perfect hostess, my sister and I happily spent all our time together.

Aparna was my aide-memoire, her photographic memory helping us paint the canvas of our peripatetic life. She would regale us with minute details from various postings, which she remembered with striking vividity.

"Remember our sampan ride with Uncle Topden to Bassein?" she asked, while I stared at her blankly.

"How can you forget? You got so sea-sick and kept throwing up."

"No wonder I don't remember," I grimaced.

"Remember how the men in Rangoon kept adjusting their lungis and we'd always wonder how they stayed in place?" giggled Aparna.

Having my sister back in my life made me realise how much I'd missed her. Once again, she became my constant companion. I'd forgotten what a chatterbox Aparna was! She talked nineteen to the dozen. No wonder she was voted the most talkative student by her eighth grade classmates in a contest held in school that year. Aparna and I had a small room each, side by side, and every night, we would call out to each other before one of us fell asleep. From my window, I would look out at Namsan Tower, dispelling iridescent colours in the distance, and I'd fall into a deep happy slumber, comforted by a warm fuzzy feeling of being home.

As usual, being in a foreign country made us giddy with excitement. Seoul felt thrilling and inviting, a large sprawling city beckoning us like a gift-wrapped box with a giant bow, just waiting for us to untie it and discover the riches concealed inside. Our house, perched halfway up Namsan Hill, was textured with yellow, brown and white stones. The external charming façade was rather deceptive; it concealed the defective inner mechanisms of the house like poor plumbing, weak water pressure, inadequate insulation, malfunctioning heating and leakages. During the bitterly cold winter months, we often found ourselves freezing in the middle of the night. The upside was it brought a delightful handyman by the name of Mr Kim to our house.

Mr Kim, like many Koreans, was full of curiosity about foreigners in his country and would ask us questions about India. While he knew about Mahatma Gandhi and Buddha, he didn't have much information about contemporary India. One day, he asked me, "Your country very poor?" I hesitated. "Some parts," I lied. I didn't want to tell him that more than half of India lived below the poverty line. I don't think Koreans would have understood why that was, given that India had gained independence from the British nearly forty years ago. Korea had taken twenty years to rise from the debris of war. While American aid had contributed to its rebuilding, many of us who had observed the Koreans knew their determination and hard work had played an even bigger role in throwing 'poverty' out of its present lexicon, into the past.

Whenever my sister and I felt homesick for India – for our extended family and the sounds of back home – we would peek out the windows and catch the shadow of the tricolour, fluttering softly and familiar, in a foreign land that was now our home.

---

This was the hedonistic eighties; music was kitsch and bubble-gum, brimming with the promise of good times. Casey Kasem became a friend who opened doors to a world of popular American culture that we lapped up. It was a sacrilege to miss his weekly Billboard Top 40 Countdown, through which Aparna and I religiously tracked our favourite numbers. Music was our high. George Michael, Prince, Phil Collins, Rick Astley, Gloria Estefan, Kylie Minogue, Duran Duran and Whitney Houston ruled our world. Our lives pulsated to the beats of *Conga* and *Walk Like an Egyptian* and infused us with aspirations. The future stretched out like a long promise. We were living the teenage dream.

It was Saturday night. Kings Club, a popular nightclub and hangout for all the GIs, was pulsating with soldiers, Korean women and several expats. I was here with Christy who had introduced me to the seedy, smoky bars of Itaewon. Christy was from Kansas and had moved to Seoul a few months earlier. Her mother worked in the Commissary and her father was an officer in the Army Infantry Division. While I was starry-eyed about Seoul, Christy complained about everything local, from the smell of garlic to the crowded buses. Her life was confined to Yongsan Base and clubbing on Saturday nights in Itaewon. Christy's primary objective in life was to find a boyfriend. The acute shortage of blonde, white American girls meant Christy was never without a date, but she was unhappy with the 'selection'.

We were standing by the bar, surveying the field, while Madonna's chartbusting single, *Material Girl*, reverberated through the packed club. I was happy to be Christy's sidekick, watching all the action from afar, except when someone asked her for a dance and she disappeared. Then, I would suffer the mortification of being on my own and waiting for her.

I spotted a Rob Lowe, with dark hair and an arresting jawline. Blue eyes were scanning the bar area, and they rested on me. Suddenly he was approaching me. I quickly downed a Coke and asked for another, and desperately wished I could evaporate. I felt awkward and shy standing at the bar by myself, and Christy seemed to have vanished, leaving me alone to face a stranger who was now just a few inches away from me.

"Hi, I'm Pete." This hunk of handsome-ness was talking to me! Just when I thought I would faint, we both heard a loud wail. It was Christy, rushing in our direction, tears streaming down her cheeks.

"Christy! What happened?" I looked at her in surprise. Just a few minutes ago she had trotted off happily with a stranger towards the dance floor. Christy was distraught, but I could see that she had registered the presence of Adonis standing beside me.

"Is everything ok?" Pete asked, looking concerned. He motioned for us to leave the club and we walked outside, the three of us, with Christy sobbing uncontrollably. She told us she had spotted her father at the neighbouring club when she'd stepped out for a smoke. And he was walking with a woman, hand in hand.

When Christy's mother found out her husband was cheating on her and romancing a local woman, she packed her bags and took Christy back with her to Kansas. Soldiers cheating on their wives were a common narrative, I discovered. Aparna's friend Jenny had the exact same experience. As quickly as Christy became part of my life, she was gone.

While I soon adjusted to my new army-college, Aparna struggled to fit into the Seoul International School, which was a culture shock after the cosy familiarity of her Air Force School back in Delhi. The eighth graders who surrounded her were not only twice her size, but were cliquish and unfriendly. Aparna's innocence and gullibility became a laughing point.

"Can you pass me the rubber?" Aparna asked a classmate timidly on her second day at school and the entire class burst out laughing.

"I was mortified," Aparna told me later. "Kids kissing and dating and stuff, I felt so out of place. Everyone had their own groups. It was such a different culture."

Among the most oversubscribed classes was one on Asian history, which attracted a large number of students. A boring three-hour lecture could have been very onerous had it not been for the presence of a Kevin Costner look-alike who made it difficult for any of the women to concentrate on the lesson. With his golden hair and sky blue eyes, he appeared blissfully oblivious to the havoc he was inflicting with his looks, and even if he were at all aware, he concealed it with élan.

On a few occasions when he sat at the desk next to mine, I was so overcome by shyness that I couldn't even look up to acknowledge him with a 'hi.' Instead, I buried my face in my book, all the while acutely conscious of his presence. One evening after class, I suddenly found him walking alongside me in the hallway.

"Hi, I'm Mark."

"Hi, er, I'm Ash." I was blushing profusely. Making eye contact was proving to be extremely difficult.

"Want to stop by Burger King? I'm starving!" he said. Before I knew it, I was walking with Kevin Costner into the fast-food chain across from our school building. He ordered a cheeseburger and I had a Coke and as we sat by the windows overlooking the parking lot, I noticed he had deep dimples that lit up his aqua eyes when he smiled. I was tongue-tied, unable to initiate any conversation. All I could do was nod while he asked me questions.

"I've been wanting to try out this Korean restaurant in Itaewon, it's got the best bulgogi in town." He looked at me enquiringly. "Want to go tomorrow night after class?"

"Um, er," I cleared my throat. I didn't even eat bulgogi, but I wasn't about to admit it. All I wanted was a chance to see him again. "Sure, I love bulgogi." *Had I just said yes to go on a date with an absolute stranger?*

The next evening Mark and I walked to the Korean restaurant after class. I noticed several women staring at him as we sat down. They were openly observing the two of us, barely able to conceal their envy.

"What's it like being in the army?" I asked. I had finally mustered enough courage and it was my turn to ask questions.

"Not too bad," said Mark. "I dropped out of college and joined the army. To tell you the truth, I needed the money. My dad put my older sis through college and funds dried up when it came to me."

"Oh," I said, thinking how very different his life was from mine. We were culturally so far apart. "I almost dropped out of college myself," I said. "Luckily we found out about the University of Maryland in Seoul and I was able to take classes here."

"Yeah," said Mark. "It's a great place. I'm grateful for this opportunity to go back to school. Korea has been an amazing experience."

"How long will you be in Seoul?" I dreaded his answer. I barely knew Mark, yet I already wanted to cling on to him.

"I'll be done next month, finishing two years here. I'm headed back to Virginia," he said. He leaned back and sighed. "I wish I'd met you earlier."

My heart did a quick somersault and my cheeks went fiery red. *I wish I had met you sooner too, I thought. This is so unfair!* There was a long silence. He looked as if he wanted to say something. Instead he picked up his fork and began tracing circles on the white tablecloth. Finally he spoke in a low voice, all the while his eyes fixed on mine. "I'm thirty-five and divorced. I have a son who lives with my ex-wife in Columbus, Ohio. My son is probably just a few years younger than you are."

He stared at me intently, waiting to see my reaction. Try as I did, I couldn't hide my expression, the shock radiating across my face. I couldn't believe what he'd told me. I had just turned nineteen, and I could've sworn Mark was in his mid- to late twenties.

"You look so young," I whispered. *Why should it matter, what's age got to do with anything, anyway?* My mind was racing as I tried to absorb the information he had just shared with me. Yet, despite his revelations, I didn't feel betrayed or disappointed. I could only think of one thing – that he was going away in a short four weeks' time and I would probably never see him again. My heart felt heavy with the ache of separation. The irrevocable truth of the matter was that I was head over heels infatuated with an American GI.

The day Mark left for Virginia, I went to drop him off at the airport. He told me I was the first Indian girl he had dated. "I'll always remember you," he said, "I'll miss you so much." I tried to fight back an avalanche of tears as we said goodbye. I watched him disappear past immigration and cried all the way back on the bus ride home. For the next several weeks I walked around weepy and heartbroken. Mark had promised he would write to me as soon as he settled in Richmond, but several weeks passed with no news from him.

At last, nearly six weeks later, a letter arrived. I tore open his letter eagerly, expecting an outpouring of emotion and longing, of how much he'd missed me. His untidy scrawl was difficult to decipher. He apologised for the delay in writing, that it had taken him a while to get adjusted to his new corporate life in the private sector. He said he had a confession to make. That during the time he had spent with me, he had also been dating Rachel, an American woman from his hometown. They had met a few times. He felt burdened by the fact that he had concealed this parallel relationship from me. Mark signed off saying he missed me and hoped our paths would cross again in the future. Mark's impersonal words were like a cold shower that jolted me out of my lovelorn slumber. I realised then that I had been just a passing fancy, one among many girls who must have thrown themselves at him. He had become my teenage dream and wrenched my heart. I wrote back, masking my anger and hurt with a casual tone informing him that I had applied to university in the States and that I would let him know once I knew which school I was headed to. Mark never wrote back and I nursed my broken pride for a long time afterwards, cursing my poor luck with romance.

---

When we got to South Korea, the country was roaring. Stunning economic growth over the past two decades had transformed this war-blighted nation into an Asian Tiger. It was also getting all dressed up to host the Asian Games and the '88 Olympics. Downtown Seoul, with its shiny high-rise buildings juxtaposed against traditional rooftops, looked like a world-class capital. The hip coffee shops of Myeong-dong, quirky bands, designer clothes, department stores, swanky offices, all pointed to a country ready for take off.

"Samsung is investing heavily in memory chips," my father informed us one evening. Despite his busy schedule, he would sometimes join the three of us for dinner and share insights about his day.

"I had a very interesting meeting with the Samsung old man this afternoon," said my father.

"You mean Mr Lee?" asked my mother, pulling a chair next to me. She poured herself a cup of tea. "Aparna, as usual, you haven't finished your vegetables."

"I *am* finishing them," said my sister, looking at me.

"Don't look at me, I'm not having your veggies," I glared at her. "Dad, what did Mr Lee say?"

"He was in a very chatty mood. What a man! What vision he has for his company and for his country," said my father. "We had a wide-ranging discussion. He talked about Nehruvian development, asked me several questions about India; he was full of curiosity and intellect."

"Is Samsung bigger than Hyundai and Daewoo?" asked Aparna. The companies were ubiquitous in South Korea, particularly on the three main television channels: KBS, KBC and MBS. They dominated the airwaves with aggressive advertising. Since they were also the sponsors of the upcoming Olympics, advertising campaigns were at a fever pitch.

"Samsung is undisputedly becoming bigger by the day," said my father. "Mr Lee was telling me about his decision to enter the semiconductor business three years back. Everyone thought it was a crazy decision, given that Samsung had absolutely no experience in this field. I asked him why he took such a risky move, especially when the Japanese were so ahead of the game, crushing everyone in memory chips – Hitachi, Toshiba, they're towering above even the Americans; they're unbeatable! Motorola, Texas Instruments, they've all ceded to the Japs."

"What did Mr Lee say?" I asked.

"His answer was short and sweet. Our dream is to beat Japan, he told me."

We all sat silent, absorbing the portent of his words. Little did we guess that in the next seven years Samsung would go on to become the number one chip manufacturer in the world.

"I'm really impressed with the nationalism of these leaders," said my mother. "They want their country to prosper, along with their companies."

"Hankuk Number One!" said my sister and I in chorus. Everyone laughed. These were the words we heard all around us constantly, *Korea Number One*, a mantra that reverberated across this country, on television, radio and among ordinary Koreans. If there was one underlying objective that fired the Koreans, it was the raw ambition to beat Japan. The pronouncement was often made with resolute certainty, without a trace of arrogance. The patriotic ardour of the average Korean struck us repeatedly. From shopkeepers to grandmothers, their desire to stand shoulder to shoulder with the world's advanced nations on an equal footing overpowered everyone. We learned the significance of the word *uri*. Coupled with *nara* (our country) it became a binding force for the Korean people, a testament to their searing nationalistic pride.

I wanted to decipher the mystifying street signs. The square, circular shapes behind which existed an exciting new linguistical world that I hungered to explore. I enrolled in Seoul National University's Korean language classes for foreigners. Sitting on the bus as it rumbled across the vast sprawl of the megapolis into the outskirts to SNU, I got glimpses of the real side of Seoul, seamy in parts, rustic in others, all engaged in a frantic race, not wanting to be left behind as waves of development washed across the city in a giant tide.

Gradually, as the weeks scrolled by, I found myself able to steer my way through the cryptic maze of Korean letters. I felt a deep flash of satisfaction when I was able to crack my very first signboard.

*Jip*. House.

As more words followed, entire conversations became possible.

*Hanguk mal arrayo?*

*Ne, chogum chogum.*

Hangul, the Korean alphabet, had become part of my life.

---

We soon discovered that being Indian in South Korea was quite a privilege. Very often Koreans would stop my mother, who wore a sari, in the middle of the road and enquire politely if she was from the land of Buddha. When she nodded, they would be delighted and immediately proceed to bow, and she would bow back in happy solidarity. Our Korean friends would often remind us of the popular legend in which an Indian princess from Ayodhya, Princess Suriratna, journeyed to Korea nearly two millenniums ago, bringing with her a message from Lord Buddha. She was said to have landed in a place called Gimhae near the present-day port town of Busan, where she married King Kim Su-ro of the Kingdom of Gimhae. The descendants of Queen Heo Hwang-ok, as she came to be subsequently known, were said to have prospered, and as a result, the people of Korea held the Princess of Ayodhya in very high regard.

As I stood in front of the memorial dedicated to Queen Heo Hwang-ok in Gimhae, I could almost visualise the beautiful princess sailing across the moonlit ocean all the way to Korea. People of Gimhae, including high-profile Koreans such as Kim Jong-pil who would later become the Prime Minister of South Korea, were very proud of their ancient lineage. On one occasion when my father had the opportunity to meet him, Kim

Jong-pil told him how he had pure blood thanks to his Indian ancestry, and said jokingly to my father, "We are from the same stock!"

---

I still had thoughts of Mark, but the passage of time helped heal my pride and broken heart. Like millions of teenage girls across the country, I too found Korean pop stars ever so romantic and developed a crush on one of them. It all happened thanks to a Korean Song Contest for Foreigners, an annual TV show that was hugely popular among Koreans in the eighties. Watching foreigners croon Korean pop songs in various accents was a source of much amusement and entertainment for ordinary Koreans who tuned in to watch the televised show in large numbers. I found myself on stage facing a packed audience in the KBS-TV studio, after a Korean friend signed me up as a contestant. Here I was, singing Ku Chang-mo's popular ballad, *Hinari*, in Korean. It felt unreal. I had a sudden déjà vu moment of a rowdy crowd in Fergusson College pelting me with tomatoes not too long ago. But unlike the college students in Pune, the audience of mostly Koreans were highly enthusiastic and encouraging and clapped wildly after I finished. I won third place in the contest, but more than the prize, the icing on the cake was the pop star himself. Ku Chang-mo was seated in the audience and when he walked on to the stage to congratulate me, and smiled his sexy smile, I swooned along with thousands of other Korean girls.

He won over my teenage heart completely.

An overseas posting was glamorous, but as usual, the Foreign Service allowance my father received was not. We were always short of cash, and Aparna and I would scrounge around the house for pocket money that we rarely got. My sister, an accountant and finance manager rolled into one, always worried about the paucity of cash in the house.

What exasperated her most was the nonchalance with which my mother and I spent the little money that we had. I really couldn't help it. The markets of Namdemum and Dongdemun were too seductive, bursting with all kinds of goodies. My mother and I, certified shopaholics, would make a beeline for the local markets because they were cheap and full of bargains, and we would return home with all kinds of things that we didn't need.

Once when Aparna saw all the soft toys in my room and the array of artificial flowers and figurines my mother had collected, she was most agitated.

"Why do you need so many things?" she admonished me, surveying all my latest purchases.

"I got great bargains," I said. Then seeing Aparna's expression, I hurriedly added, "I swear, I didn't spend *that* much."

"Did you know that on my school field trip last month I boiled ramen in the room every night while the others ate at restaurants? That's how careful I am, and here you and Mom are busy buying junk!"

"It's not junk," I said defensively.

"You know, I heard Dad saying he's already run out of money and there's a big delegation coming next week," said my sister who kept a sharp eye on the official goings-on and knew which Minister from India was arriving when. She thought of various strategies to draw my father's attention to the financial plight at home and to rein in his spendthrift wife and daughter. She finally came up with a plan.

A few days later, my father returned from work in the evening, grinning from ear to ear. A letter had arrived for him at the embassy. It was a formal complaint stating that the Ambassador's wife Alka and his older daughter were causing a domestic cash crunch. The matter was of utmost urgency, since funds were no longer available for the younger daughter to spend on her school requirements. This extravagance should be curbed immediately, the letter declared, to pre-empt the Ambassador from bankruptcy. At the bottom, Aparna had signed her name with a flourish.

We all had a hearty laugh and needless to say, that month my sister was given generous pocket money for the first time, which she promptly and politely declined.

---

The deluge of Indian delegations began soon after my parents arrived in Seoul. Stories about South Korea's stunning economic success had been making the rounds in India. Officials, always ready for a foreign trip, began descending upon us in droves. It was the responsibility of the embassy staff to look after them, so each time a delegation came to town, my parents would host receptions for them; they really didn't have a choice but to roll out the welcome mat for these dignitaries because displeasing any of these VVIPs would be akin to inflicting self-injury.

Since it was too expensive to take them to restaurants, the

brunt of entertaining these officials at home fell squarely on my mother, her two assistants (my sister and me) and our cook from India who kept threatening to leave. Our house would turn into a mini restaurant. Hundreds of *samosas* and *gulab jamuns* would line the kitchen counters, along with *tandoori* chicken.

After slogging it out in the kitchen, my mother would dash to her room to don her sari and reappear, elegant and charming, just in time to usher in the guests. She really need not have bothered because the visiting officials were far more interested in the food; they would straightaway make a beeline for the buffet table, and some would even forget to thank the hostess afterwards!

Hosting a formal dinner was like conducting an orchestra, my mother would joke. The local Korean waiters – many of them had never see Indian food before – would be utterly confused by the array of dishes and the sequence they were required to follow. My mother would write down the name of each dish in big bold letters and explain in detail when to produce it at the table. The *dal* and rice must come together and the *aloo* and *poori* should follow, she would tell them with a lot of sign language since none of them could speak English. "They would nod at everything I said," recounted my mother. "But actually they hadn't understood a single word!"

Strict protocol had to be followed for such dinners. This meant that when everyone was seated, no one could leave the table, including the host and hostess, until the end of the meal. "I felt trapped," my mother would tell us. "I'd be dying to get up and supervise what was going on in the kitchen, I knew there was pandemonium inside!"

During one official dinner, my mother was seated at the far end of the table, flanked by two ministers. From the corner of her eye, she saw one of the Korean waiters walk in, carrying rice and *poori* in each hand. With a big smile on his face, he placed the two dishes in front of the Korean Trade Minister. To my mother's horror, the Minister started to stuff his *poori* with the rice and proceeded to eat it with great gusto.

"I didn't know what to do, I could only look on helplessly," my mother groaned in recollection. "I wanted to tell him to dip the *poori* in the *aloo sabji* (potato vegetable), and have the rice with the curry, but he was sitting too far away from me!" Such faux pas were common at dinner parties. If a sit-down meal ended without any major gaffes, my mother would disintegrate with relief. "I couldn't remember any conversations I had with my guests during the dinner, I was so focused on what the waiters were doing!" she would say. Once when a minister from India fell asleep at the table, she didn't know whether to laugh or cry.

---

My sister and I steered clear of our parents' official parties, but every now and then my mother would rope me in to usher in the guests and ensure they were looked after, which I would do reluctantly.

The Indian Republic Day reception was in full swing. The house was decked with candles and flowers. The evening tinkled with the clink of glasses, laughter and conversation, as prominent people with fleeting attention spans, stood around in clusters.

"Brenda, meet my daughter," my mother introduced me to the Belgian diplomat's wife.

"Hello, how nice to meet you." The lady, who was immaculately dressed, offered me a limp handshake.

"Ashwini is studying Korean at Seoul National University," my mother said.

"Oh, that's very nice, how long have you been studying there?" she asked. Before I could reply, the woman turned to my mother and said in a low voice, "Have you met the new Foreign Minister's wife? I believe some of the Ambassadors' wives have met her; I hear she doesn't give appointments easily, she's quite reclusive." She waved a bangled arm in the air, "Alka, your house looks so lovely tonight," and moved on to talk to the next person. These were people who had perfected the art of small talk; in some ways I envied them.

"What's the point of such parties?" I'd ask my mother. "No one is really interested in listening to what you have to say. Everyone is busy looking through each other! It's *so* artificial!"

"Don't be so anti-social," my mother would say to Aparna and me. "Both of you should learn to mingle a bit, this is how you get to know and meet people."

"Right," we laughed. Thanks to my mother's overflowing hospitality, we hosted hundreds of guests in our home over the years; many of whom would scarcely recognise her when she ran into them back in Delhi. But my mother's enthusiasm never wavered. She didn't let the underlining artifice of relationships in the Foreign Service dent her positive spirit or make her cynical.

In the mid-eighties, South Korea was convulsed in student demonstrations against the authoritarian, military regime of Chun Doo-hwan. Student protests, an intrinsic part of Korean political life, were shaping and defining the pro-democracy movement. I would often hear references to the Kwangju massacre in hushed conversations. Two years before we arrived in Seoul, government troops fired on civilians, mostly students, in the city of Kwangju, killing nearly two hundred and brutally crushing the pro-democracy movement. The incident, known as the Kwangju massacre, sparked nationwide outrage and proved to be a lightning rod in South Korea's march for democracy.

One morning, my father reached the embassy earlier than usual. He settled into his room, scanned through the newspapers and was reaching out for his cup of tea when he happened to glance outside his window. To his shock, he saw a massive crowd of students gathered across the road, where the entrance of Dankook University was located.

"What's happening outside Dankook?" my father asked his officer, Third Secretary Mr Malhotra.

"Sir, it's a student protest. Nothing to worry about."

"Nothing to worry about?" my father looked at Malhotra in disbelief.

"Yes, Sir; we are quite safe, I checked with Foreign Ministry, they assured us there is no danger to us. We don't need to leave the office, Sir."

My father was a bit sceptical, but it turned out that Malhotra was right. For the next several hours, my father and his officers watched the scene evolve as the students took their positions in the street below. Within minutes, the police arrived, carrying batons and shields. Loud cries of "Down with Chun!" echoed through Hannam-dong, as the students shouted slogans and waved banners.

As the protests continued throughout the morning, the police remained restrained, watching without retaliating. By afternoon, the crowds of students had swelled and become rowdy; they began hurling Molotov cocktails. The police swung into action and fired teargas, the effects of which could be felt by the embassy staff huddled in their offices above, rubbing their itching teary eyes. The teargas did the trick, and within minutes, the students began to disperse. By 5pm, the demonstration was over. Everything returned to normal.

"Sir, *rasta clear hai*," informed Mr Malhotra, who had been continuously in touch with the Foreign Ministry throughout the day. "The students will be back tomorrow, Sir, same time as today."

The student protests continued all week, in the same precise orderly manner, beginning around 9am and ending by 5pm. As my father returned home each evening that week, he marvelled at the spirit and determination of the students. They refused to be mowed down.

This was just the beginning of a tide of unrest that swept across the country. Over the next few weeks, the protests spiralled out of control, including the one at Dankook University opposite the Indian Embassy, as thousands of civilians showed solidarity with the students, calling for immediate political reform. That's when my father decided to fortify the entrance of the embassy with a double glass door.

With the Olympic Games around the corner, the last thing

the government wanted was a surge in student radicalism. Crushing the pro-democracy movement no longer became a viable option for Chun Doo-hwan. The movement was growing stronger by the day, even as the countdown for the biggest show on earth was about to take place.

Unable to hold out to the international and domestic pressure around him, the President announced his resignation on June 30, 1987, and the embracing of full democracy in South Korea. The jubilation that echoed around the country found its way into our home, and while my sister and I danced around the house in celebration, my parents watched, in stupefied wonder, the historic developments on television.

A year later, South Korea hosted the Olympics and its first free parliamentary elections.

---

In the fall of 1988, the Seoul Sports Complex located on the southern side of the Han River, became the scene for the country's most spectacular sporting event. The South Koreans had been gearing up for this event for years, wanting their spot on the global stage. So keen were they to impress visiting foreigners that even rooftops were painted in bright colours to welcome those flying into the country.

Since Japan had hosted the Games in 1964, the South Koreans were impatient not to be left behind; they became the second Asian country to host the Olympics. Japan's use of the Games as a springboard for international fame and recognition was fresh in the minds of most South Koreans who wanted the event to foster the same miracle for them as it had for Japan in the 1960s.

Hodori, the bubbly smiling tiger mascot, bounced around Olympic Park, spreading its cheerful bonhomie among the thousands of visitors and athletes. As a volunteer, I too shared the thrill of having a ringside view to the world's most extraordinary athletes, united by a singular objective: to make their country proud, to smash old records and attain glory. Every day we were witness to goosebump moments that would echo across the city of Seoul and reverberate around the world: Carl Lewis awarded the 100m gold after Canadian Ben Johnson was stripped of his medal for using drugs; American diver Greg Louganis winning a gold for his flawless reverse somersaults while diving off the 3-metre springboard – that too after he'd hit his head on the board during a preliminary round, and received stitches. It was a testament to the triumph of human endurance.

The South Korean athletes did astonishingly well, which came as no surprise. They took sixth place in the medal tally led by the USSR and the US. India's three-hundred-strong delegation went home with one medal. As I walked around the sports venues, looking at the flags of the 159 nations fluttering in the afternoon breeze, I felt a rush of pride for this country with its indomitable can-do spirit that had allowed it to battle the odds and achieve the impossible.

---

Like my host country, I too was ready to take flight. I'd just turned 21 and had graduated from the University of Maryland. America loomed like El Dorado on my horizon. The future was full of promise. I was off to pursue my Master's Degree in

Journalism in the United States. As my flight readied for take off, I peered outside the window, eyes blurring as I bid goodbye to my parents, my sister and a country I had grown to love.

Author reporting for Prince George's Television, 1994

# Guns and Graffiti

## USA
*1990s*

## Maryland

It was the era of big hair and even bigger shoulder pads, and mine were *enormous*. I still haven't figured out the equation between the shoulder pads and gravitas, but the ratings seemed to suggest they worked. So there I was, in a nicely padded navy suit, with a yellow satin shirt that gave me this golden girl glow and my billowing hair, which could edge me gently out of my anchor chair in a Mary Poppins rise towards the sky. I had selected a pair of earrings that complimented my buttery shirt just right. They were rather large golden orbs, somewhat concealed by my voluminous hair, which glittered in the studio light like fireflies.

We were a minute to air. I did a quick check in my compact mirror, made sure my nose wasn't shiny and no hair was sticking out funny.

"Three two one, you're on-air."

I read through the voice-over script in my broadcast voice, deepened or lightened according to the story. The navy suit worked well for the hard-hitting stories; I just automatically slipped into serious mode. As I began reading an intro to a package, a reverberating sound echoed through the studio – and across the county it felt like. For a nano second I was completely disoriented. Where was the sound coming from? Almost instantly, I realised to my horror that my earring had fallen off and was bounding on the wooden platform where the anchor desk stood, before clattering across the floor. The teleprompter operator froze, while I felt a momentary loss of sensation in my limbs. With some help from high above, I managed to finish the sentence I was reading, keeping my face stoic. Luckily we went into a taped package. There was a shocked silence in the gallery before the director came on. "What the heck was that?"

"My earring fell off," I said sheepishly, before loud guffaws from the gallery drowned my mortified whimpers.

"Are you serious?" laughed Bert, the technical director, darting into the studio before the package ended, to check on me.

My News Director Dave found it much less funny. "Next time, ditch the earrings please," was all he said.

---

How on earth did I, a foreigner from India, land up in one of Washington, DC's grittiest suburbs, covering the crime beat?

It was the summer of 1990. I had graduated from the American University, Washington, with a Master's Degree in Broadcast Journalism. Now I needed to find a job quickly. Make that *urgently*. In a few months' time my international student visa was going to expire and I'd have to go back to India. But I couldn't really share my panic with any of my classmates. For one thing, a majority of them were Americans who had no clue what an F-1 or H1B visa was. I was cautious about opening up to them, because even though the Cold War had officially ended, I fretted that they would brand me a communist if they discovered my place of birth was Russia.

"It's not looking good," I called Aparna, who was studying international relations at the Jawaharlal Nehru University in

Delhi. "In fact, it's not looking good *at all*."

"It's not so bad here in India, you know," Aparna was saying. Her soothing maturity was like a place of refuge in a storm. But she was so far away, her voice sounded so remote. I felt horribly homesick.

"You could easily get a job here," she was saying. "Some private channels are starting up. They would surely love to hire you."

The thought of going back to India and working for the state-run channel Doordarshan was not the gilded career path I was aspiring for. I'd come all the way to America to study and work, and had every intention of sticking it out, even if it meant knocking on a hundred doors. Besides, I had fallen in love with the verdant environs of Washington, DC, and the luxury of anonymity that came from living alone in America. Life was a bit too heady to give up just yet.

It didn't help that America was in the grip of a frightening recession, and in the downturn, the job market had become a bleak, dank place. The press was full of news of gloomy economic outlooks and plummeting consumer confidence. The Savings and Loans Crisis and the Persian Gulf War were taking its toll on the economy, which was hitting rock bottom growth. Crime was soaring across the DC metropolitan area, making the capital one of the most lethal places in the country.

As my Master's programme in Broadcast Journalism came to an end, I became aware of a grave mismatch – my career ambition to be a television reporter clashed with the reality of my being an accented foreigner. As far as I could see, there were no Fresh-Off-the-Boat Indians on mainstream American television. Most of the other Indian students I knew were studying either engineering or economics. The irrevocable truth was that, to go *on-air*, you had to sound American and dunk yourself into the culture. That's about the time I decided to perfect the 'twang'. Without the American accent you would remain a 'foreigner' till eternity. Roll those *r*'s nice and round, and start saying *dance* and *can't* the American way. For a long time I'd say *cannot* instead of *can't*, simply because I couldn't get myself to saying *can't* without sounding utterly fake. Faking an accent can imply that you are trying to be someone you are not. In other words, you are tampering with your *identity*. An accent would not have been an impediment in other fields, but in broadcast news, sounding foreign was anathema, with a capital A. Once I accepted that I would *have* to sound 'fake', I felt liberated. It was a survival instinct. I gathered all my ego, pride, patriotism, nationalism and threw them out the window. Now was not the time to wade in immigrant mush.

During my job search, I discovered there existed something called the 100 Television Markets, ranked by population: a listing of the top news stations in the United States. These were the affiliates of the four giant networks in the US – namely, ABC, NBC, CBS and Fox. All television hopefuls, including myself, would pore over these rankings, enviously looking at the elusive top 100, the Ivy League news stations in the country. This venerated bracket included New York, LA, Chicago, Philadelphia and other big cities, while those from 101 and below were obscure middle-of-nowhere places like Corpus Christi, Zanesville, Hagerstown and Amarillo, where rookie reporters like myself were supposed to get started. 'Paying your dues' was the dreaded buzzword in every reporter's lexicon.

Having scaled the citadel of higher education, I was confident this would automatically place me at the top of the pecking order for employment. This myth was quickly busted as I embarked on my job search and discovered no one spared a breath to a master's degree. All that mattered was whether I had done a live shot, covered a fire or a local election and had a montage of my work, outside of what I'd done in school. That field experience would triumph over academic scholarship was a startling revelation. I was politely told that I was 'overqualified'. How on earth was I to explain that to my parents? That I'd spent all their hard-earned money on a degree just to be told I was *overqualified* for the job! I felt myself sinking under the weight of the irony.

Money was running out. I couldn't dream of asking my father to send me any. My parents were reeling under the bombshell of a posting order to Chernobyl-struck Ukraine, where everything was going to be in short supply including food and housing. They worried about the effects of radiation, which had already got one of their colleagues very ill. The last thing they needed was to hear about my financial troubles. I would have to manage on the small bit of cash left in my rapidly diminishing bank account. Even the part-time job I had in the college computer lab, which went towards my rent, had ended the day I graduated.

I started making phone calls and sent my tapes scattershot to obscure stations across the country. Several weeks and endless rejections later, I got a solitary response from an NBC affiliate down south for an interview. It sounded extremely promising, except the NBC affiliate was in Texas! Virginia was the farthest south I'd ever travelled; I had butterflies in my stomach at the prospect of heading to what seemed like another country.

I fully and solidly bombed the interview. For one thing, I appeared and sounded utterly foreign. Sitting inside the News

Director's bright, airy office, looking out at the corn fronds swaying in the breeze, I was gripped by a surreal sense of incredulity. What on earth was I doing at this NBC station in *Lubbock, Texas*, explaining to this stranger that I was born in Moscow, had lived in South Korea and was an Indian with an H1B visa? My tryst with small town America ended the minute I stumbled out of the door.

"I had the worst job interview ever in Texas," I called Aparna later that night.

"In *Texas*? Have you gone nuts?"

"I don't have a choice, it's not like NBC and ABC are rolling out the red carpet for me, you know. Can you believe CNN in Atlanta said they have no jobs and PBS has a hiring freeze? But guess what, I have an interview in Hagerstown next week."

"Where?"

"Hagerstown. It's in Maryland."

"What are you going to do if you don't find anything?"

"Go to Plan B."

"And what's Plan B?"

"I don't have one."

I realised in a panic that I had only three months left before my visa expired.

---

The one-year lease on the room I was renting was ending soon and I would be glad never to see my roommates again. Both the American girls had swindled me into sharing their two-bedroom apartment with them. Exploiting my lack of money and my immigrant status, they offered me the walk-in closet (thankfully it was spacious) as my room, and made me pay the same rent to boot. It was a lesson in humiliation of Herculean magnitude that I swallowed for a year, seething every time I walked past Kristy and Laura's expansive, sunlit rooms crammed with every conceivable item that anyone could possibly need, from food to clothes to plants to books to rugs and mirrors. Meanwhile my narrow, windowless space (I refused to call it a room) had just about enough area to accommodate a single mattress and a small bookshelf. Many an immigrant's tribulations I had heard of, but I never expected to experience such mortification myself.

Just when I thought my life was a series of jump cuts, the sun peeked through the clouds and spilled some sunshine onto my life. I got an interview call from a community channel in Prince George's County, a suburb of Washington, DC. PG County was an outlier, sitting on the other side of the Beltway. It would have, in all probability, remained anonymous, had it not been for its spiralling crime rate that had propelled it to national prominence. PG County earned the notoriety of having the maximum murders that year, beating the national average by a mile, thereby becoming the *enfant terrible* of the DC metro area. The only reason I'd heard of the place was because that's where all the *murders* and *drug busts* occurred. It was pure lunacy to consider working in such a neighbourhood. In my family, I was not known for bravery. The sight of a lizard was enough to reduce me to quivering jelly. I liked my comfort zone a bit too much and was not one to seek adventure. Hesitation and diffidence often defined me. Yet, here I was, trying to bungee jump even though I was terrified of heights.

How would I get to Prince George's County? I didn't know how to drive and didn't own a car, and there was no public transport of any kind, as far as I knew, that went that far.

My meeting with the News Director was a success. At the end of our conversation, Dave Hummel told me he could only offer me a 'volunteer' position, at least to begin with. "Budget cuts," he explained.

*Budget cuts, hiring freeze, recession, lay-offs*, these words were like the reprise of a dirge that kept choking me. I swallowed my disappointment.

"It's the only way for you to get your foot in the door," Dave continued.

I nodded.

"I hope you will consider joining our team," he said.

"It would be my privilege," I heard myself saying.

*Oh my God, I had just shackled myself to American suburbia for the next five years.*

---

Riding the metro twenty-five miles out to Prince George's County proved to be a nerve-wracking experience. On the first day, I got a whiff of the sinister. I tentatively got on the Orange Line, which tunnelled through the sprawl of the Washington metropolitan area, stretching from northern Virginia on one end to Maryland on the other, in an hour-long ride. It was rush hour and the train was packed to the brim with office-goers. Half an hour into the ride, the train pulled into Capital South in downtown Washington, where a large number of government offices are located, including the US Capitol. As the train came to a stop, the passengers rose in one choreographic sweep and the train emptied out. I realised, in a surge of panic, that I was the sole passenger left in the carriage and possibly in the entire train. I looked around at the empty seats as the train started again, crossing the Anacostia River into Southeast DC, which had recently been declared as the most dangerous place to live in the entire country and the reason why Washington, DC had acquired the ignominious distinction of being labelled as the nation's crime capital.

I had a sinking, eerie feeling as I sat by the window, staring outside at the scenery which was starting to change dramatically. The prosperity of Washington receded; barbed wire, litter and boarded-up homes came into view juxtaposed with liquor stores and graffiti walls. As we crossed the border into Prince George's, the communities became more and more impoverished, it was a desolate landscape. We came to Deanwood Station. I was oblivious to the fact that the station had recently been the site of a spate of killings.

A man got in. I noticed him from the corner of my eye, and saw to my dismay that he was walking in my direction. The intuitive sixth, seventh and eighth sense every woman has, when she can sniff out a predator from a mile away, made me move to the next seat, so he wouldn't be able to sit next to me. He came up to my seat and stood right beside me, even though the entire carriage was empty. I instinctively drew my elbows inwards and clutched my bag, all the while looking out of the window, praying fervently that he wasn't carrying a gun or a knife. He started to whistle.

"Hi," he said. He was close enough for me to smell the alcohol. His whistling grew louder, while I tried to quell the waves of dread that were cascading through my body. At that moment, I heard my station being announced and I jumped out of my seat. Pushing past him, I ran through the sliding doors as fast as I could, down the escalators and out of the station, not daring to look over my shoulder. All the while my legs were threatening to give way. The station was completely deserted, as was the bus stop, with the next bus that would take me to the office due in five minutes. Once again, I was the only passenger on the bus and during the ten-minute ride I vowed that before the month was up, I would be driving my way to work.

Within a month, I was offered a permanent reporter position at Prince George's Television. During my trial period, I managed to get a friend to teach me driving and practised furiously every evening after I got home from work. I was desperate. The fear of getting back on that empty train fired me with a determination that propelled me to clear the driving test in two weeks. On my meagre salary, which was just about enough to cover my rent for a studio apartment in Arlington, I got myself a second-hand car, which spluttered me to work for the next five years.

---

It was an era of typewriters, three-quarter inch tapes and landlines. We worked out of a cramped newsroom, which was just big enough to accommodate four desks. Our skeletal team was helmed by Dave Hummel, the News Director who had made it his hallmark to incorporate human-interest stories alongside crime news. Dave was meticulous about the stories we covered; his perseverance and tenacity were hard to combat, as was his equanimity, which earned him respect in the journalism fraternity. My two fellow reporters, Mandy and Sue, were young, hungry and ambitious, and I knew it was only a matter of time before they jumped ship to the bigger, more glamorous local channels. Jim, the chief cameraman, was a big guy with wild hair and a gentle demeanour; his amiable and cheerful personality helped pull everyone through the spate of dismal news we kept getting day after day.

"Ash, we've got a double homicide. I need you to package it." It was my third day on the job. The only packages I had ever done were for my television production classes in college. While I knew the nuts and bolts of putting together a package, this was the *real world*.

"You mean, package it, like in get interviews and do a stand-up?" I stuttered slightly.

That was the wrong thing to say. Dave looked annoyed. "Yes, that's exactly what I meant. You will need to do a stand-up. Jim and you need to leave now! The cops are already on the way. 400 block of Laurel Avenue. Now *go*!"

Jim and I rushed to the scene, my mind spinning in a thousand directions. How should I package a homicide? Who would I interview? Would I have to see the bodies?

As our van turned into the block, we saw that a small crowd had gathered at the end of the street. A yellow ribbon had cordoned off the crime scene, indicating police presence. On the edge of the street was a body, with a police investigator standing next to it, taking notes. A few feet away, another body lay slumped on the sidewalk. Double homicide. Trying to mask my shock at seeing the corpses, I looked at Jim who was already rolling.

"Give me a white balance," he said. Noticing my expression, he patted my shoulder. "Don't worry, you will get used to this real fast." Surely, it would take me months to acquire that analgesic layer essential for covering the crime beat.

"You wanna do a stand-up quickly, before the bodies are removed?" Jim asked.

"Er, you mean, here, now?" I said, feeling extremely nervous.

"Yeah, hon, go for it, we don't have much time," said Jim.

I quickly scripted my stand-up and did it in two takes. Jim gave me the thumbs-up. "Nice job, Ash."

"Thanks Jim," I said, relieved the stand-up was over. The stand-up was a key component of a news report where the viewer got to see the reporter. A poorly delivered stand-up could make or break even the most solid news piece.

I looked around for a police officer to get some information about the murders. "The cops seem so busy, I don't want to disturb them," I said hesitatingly to Jim.

He looked at me and grinned. "Ash, you gotta push your way in there and ask your questions, don't be shy! Come on, let me introduce you to Mark. He's the Police Press Officer; he's a real nice guy. We interview him all the time, he knows the drill."

Jim was right. Mark was friendly and helpful and instantly put me at ease. He explained what he knew of the double homicide. "One 20-year-old male shot in the head. Both suspects appear to have been involved in an altercation that led to shots being fired. We believe this to be a drug-related crime. It appears to be all about retribution."

Fifteen seconds' soundbite, nice and tight. Wouldn't need much editing back in the studio. Jim taught me how to time code interviews, an indispensable tool for field reporting which was a lifesaver when it was down to the wire in the edit suite. I felt hugely grateful to Jim. Without his handholding I might have missed out on several key elements of the story.

I still managed to come back to the station without all the information.

"So, how many homicides does that take us to this year in Prince George's?" Dave wanted to headline the number. I looked at him blankly.

"Er, I, I don't know, I'm sorry, I, er, forgot to ask," I said, my heart sinking, feeling like a school kid who had forgotten to turn in my homework. I had come back without a vital piece of information.

One eyebrow shot up. Dave did *not* look pleased. He pursed his lips. "Well, you better call the police department ASAP and get the number for me." I wanted to hide under my desk in embarrassment.

I discovered "*What bleeds, leads*" was the mantra in local news. Under Dave's boot camp, I learnt the ropes of news reporting in small-town USA. Accurate information gathering while out in the field was at the heart of being a smart, successful reporter. Dave was a straight shooter who did not mince words. He did not approve of flowery writing – long winding sentences and multiple adjectives were out. Our scripts had to be crisp and clear. One idea per sentence. "Where's the lead? Don't bury the lead!" Dave would admonish us. Under his mentorship, Sue, Mandy and I learnt to write punchy headlines and sharp scripts. We learnt to crosscheck and double-check our facts and numbers. We learnt to keep our opinions out and balance the news by presenting both sides of the story. Accuracy, Attribution and Objectivity were the three cornerstones of Dave's newsroom.

I became the queen of stand-up's. I learnt to carry the tripod, to script while driving back from a shoot and to edit my own pieces. Sometimes we would be editing our package five minutes to air. The frantic pace of daily news was exhilarating; my life became a dizzying loop of soundbites and stand-ups.

Press conferences were my nemesis, where you had to ask questions. For the first few pressers, I was too mortified to raise my hand, too timid to ask a question that might make me look stupid in full view of the Washington press corps. When I returned to the station without a soundbite, I had to once again face Dave's disapproval. "Tentativeness has no place in a newsroom," he said. From that day onwards, I began asking questions at press conferences without worrying if they sounded intelligent or not. The satisfaction of having my question answered in a room packed with reporters from the big networks gave me immense satisfaction. I was slowly but steadily paying my dues.

---

I snipped off my frizzy hair and acquired the broadcast bob. I invested in several business suits. My two bibles were the *NBC Handbook of Pronunciation* and the *AP Writer's Handbook*, which I consulted diligently. Within six months, I was co-anchoring the evening news alongside Dave. While going *live* for the first time was terrifying, sitting beside Dave on the anchor desk was a privilege I was grateful for.

I learnt to hide my international background, because *local* mattered. The team at PGTV became the family I did not have in America. From the onset, they welcomed me into their fold, treating me with affection and respect. We forged close bonds while working side by side, sharing stories about our lives, bantering and joking with one another that helped foster an informal atmosphere in the newsroom. While everyone at the station was vaguely aware of my foreign roots and was cognisant of the existence of India, it remained for them a very distant land which blinked somewhere out there in the universe. America had chopped a 'poor' stamp on India so firmly, it was difficult for them to fathom it was a vibrant democracy with bright, intelligent people. If at all, they might have felt empathy for me, that I had 'escaped' and come to America, to this golden land which gave industrious Third World citizens like me a path to forge a new destiny.

I was on the road to assimilation.

---

The world was experiencing cataclysmic change. The free currents of perestroika and glasnost swirled in the air. A few months later the Berlin Wall crumbled, and in China, thousands of demonstrating students were arrested in Tiananmen Square. Back home in India, curfews were enforced following the Mandal Commission's reservation policy of jobs for the backward classes that unleashed a storm of outrage across the nation.

But in Prince George's County, we remained in a penumbra. We were unaffected by the global headwinds, despite being a half hour away from the capital city of the most powerful nation on earth.

I felt disembodied from my past as a globetrotting diplomat's daughter. It seemed to have little relevance to my life as a local reporter in the United States. There wasn't anything in my surroundings to remind me of the places I had once lived in, including India. Not wanting to be cast as a foreigner became my single-minded focus, a form of self-preservation, as I tried to establish my credentials in the newsroom. Greenbelt, Landover, Hyattsville, Temple Hills, Upper Marlboro, Suitland and Annapolis were my new points of reference, my new geography, as Jim and I drove around the county interviewing people and gathering footage for the evening news. Involuntarily, I would find myself gravitating towards stories from Asia. A few months into my job when a major story tore India apart, I was emotionally drawn to the events in my homeland.

It was the summer of 1991. One morning, on a slow news day, I'd been trying to get my head around a complicated state education bill that was being proposed by some lawmakers in Annapolis. I happened to look up at the TV screen in our newsroom and saw a breaking news chyron flash across the monitor. CNN was airing a big story out of India. I watched in stunned silence as the anchor announced that India's 47-year-old former Prime Minister Rajiv Gandhi had been assassinated while on the campaign trail in the south. I stood up and walked to the monitor, transfixed, as the reality of the tragedy sank in. I could feel the after-shocks right there in our newsroom, light years away from the streets of New Delhi, as I watched Rajiv Gandhi's funeral procession.

Just at that moment, Jim strolled into the newsroom, and upon seeing my face, he immediately knew something was amiss. "What's up?" he asked. I explained to him that India was in turmoil, and the man whom I believed would take India into the modern age, was dead, his dreams of modernising India turned to debris. That afternoon we interviewed more people from the Indian community than we could accommodate; people were so saddened by Rajiv Gandhi's death, they spoke passionately and straight from their hearts. I put together a lengthy package, using the opportunity to weave in some background about India's Congress Party that had ruled the country since the end of the British rule. Dave was so struck by the story that he suggested I get a live guest for our broadcast. That evening, many residents in Prince George's County followed the journey of a dynamic, promising man whose destiny had turned to rubble in a grisly instant. They too felt the ripples of the profound sadness and horror that gripped the subcontinent, millions of miles away from their world.

---

I had been working in Prince George's County for three years. I learnt to combat homesickness by clocking long hours at work. Unlike most of the others who had family in the area, I didn't have anyone to go home to. My sister had long given up trying to get me to return to India. "How long are you planning to do this?" Aparna would ask. I could feel her concern through the static of our poor connection. "Another year, and I'll quit," I told her, convinced I wouldn't survive suburbia a day longer.

When I'd saved enough money, I bought myself a ticket to visit my parents in Kiev. Ravaged by communism, the conditions in newly independent Ukraine were depressing. Kiev was poor and run-down with crumbling facilities, dilapidated buildings, empty stores and beggars. My parents, cooped up in two small hotel rooms for a year and a half before the embassy acquired a property and established an official presence in the country, were struggling to find normalcy under very difficult conditions. They had converted one of their two rooms into a kitchen, where my mother cooked on a stove. Within a few months of their arrival, the Indian President visited Ukraine and the pressure of official entertainment once again fell on my mother's shoulders. My parents were reminded of their days of hardship in Moscow, but Ukraine was even worse because of the danger of Chernobyl, which was just a hundred kilometres from Kiev. The fear of radiation lurked all around them. While other European diplomats would leave the country frequently to avoid continuous exposure to radiation, my parents could not afford the travel. Even bottled water was believed to be contaminated and not considered safe to drink. I worried about my parents' well-being; two years later, when my father was told he was being transferred back to Delhi, I felt a big boulder had been lifted off my shoulders.

I continued to hunger for foreign news which I found intoxicating. Having lived in America for so long, it was easy to forget there was a universe out there, called the *Rest of the World*. And that this foreign universe was populated with other countries and television channels. Every once in a while my Indian friends would watch cricket on Sky TV or Star News, the two popular channels in the nineties that came on obscure cable platforms, or catch 'real news' as they called it, on the BBC, which they revered, but few Americans were aware of. But how could I infuse any international flavour into our programming? I pitched the idea of a talk show to Dave, who agreed to let me do a monthly half-hour programme focusing on global issues.

'The World Mirror' was born. Suddenly I was interacting with embassies in Washington, the World Bank, the IMF, universities and think tanks. I began reaching out to Indian friends who were working in the DC area; many of them were now at international organisations.

I called up Kaushik, who used to live in my neighbourhood in Delhi. He had recently graduated from Georgetown and was working at the World Bank. I was reconnecting with old friends and it made me realise just how much I'd missed them.

"Kaushik, I need a favour. I'm looking for guests to feature on my talk show. The topic is immigration and integration."

Kaushik vaguely knew that I was working for some TV station. "You do a talk show?" he asked, sounding impressed.

"Ya, sort of," I said. I was used to most of my Indian friends' lack of familiarity with the world of broadcast journalism, especially local news.

"Where's your office?" asked Kaushik.

"We have a studio in Prince George's County."

"Prince George's County?" Kaushik sounded horrified. I don't blame him. He was not unlike many other friends of mine, who had never crossed the Anacostia River to the 'other side'. They preferred to live inside the Beltway, in the safe cocoons of Roslyn or Bethesda. "Wow, you're brave."

"I want to feature both FOBs and ABCDs." Indians freely used these acronyms to describe which category they fell into. Fresh-off-the-Boat were typically the newly arrived students, while the American-born-Confused-Desi represented the second generation of Indians whose parents had immigrated back in the fifties and sixties.

"Kaushik, you are the perfect FOB. Please come on my show."

"Are you mad? Not me, but I have the perfect candidate for you. He's a very chatty guy, I think he's your man."

Kaushik's words were prophetic. Not only would Manish be the chattiest guest on my show, he would end up becoming my husband. But of course, neither one of us knew that at the time.

We taped 'The World Mirror' at night, following the evening news. Manish, Sonia, Meera and Anil arrived at the station, the first time they had ventured to this part of town. They looked bewildered as they walked into the studio.

"Wow, this place is amazing," said Anil. "How long have you worked here?"

"Coming up to four years," I said. I lapped up their attention; it had been so long since Indian men had paid me any.

The newly arrived Indians spoke freely about their futures, which they believed would flourish in America. Did they miss India? Were they planning to go back eventually?

"This is the land of opportunity, there's no doubt about that," said Manish. "Of course, I do miss so many aspects of home, but for now, I do foresee myself living and working in this country."

The challenges of integration were a common thread, binding both groups. The ABCDs spoke about conflicting identities and the perennial struggle to balance their traditional Indian roots with the onslaught of Western modernity they faced outside of their homes.

"The goal of every immigrant should be not to just co-exist, but to integrate into the community," said Manish.

We spoke for an hour, a free-flowing conversation, as if we were sitting comfortably in our living room and forgot all about the cameras. As Kaushik had predicted, Manish was at his chattiest best. He was articulate and animated and the show was a grand success.

In September of 1992, the Governor of Arkansas, Bill Clinton, brought his presidential campaign to Maryland, and I was the reporter assigned to cover the story. With the elections just nine weeks away, there was heightened euphoria about Clinton's visit, given his soaring popularity in Maryland.

On the day of the event, Jim and I reached the community college in Rockville well in time to set up. A large crowd had gathered in the outdoor arena, eager to hear what the Governor had to say. When Clinton walked in, the crowd burst into loud cheers and applause. Looking every bit presidential, Clinton mesmerised the crowd with his boyish looks and charisma. He struck an instant rapport with the students, emphasising that economic growth could only be achieved through investment in education. He took several punches at his opponent George Bush. "They believe that you make the economy grow by putting money first. I believe you make an economy grow by putting people first!"

The crowd roared back in approval. This rally was seen as a bellwether for the campaign; Clinton would go on to defeat Bush squarely in the upcoming elections. It was an extraordinary comeback for the Democrats, breaking twelve years of Republican dominance.

Five years later, local news was beginning to choke me with its noose of fires, homicides and county council elections. I could feel the knot tightening every day, as I drove fifty miles to and from the office. Doing stand-ups in the middle of pumpkin patches during Halloween and chasing cops for the latest crime statistics had lost its lustre. The violence around me was also beginning to take its toll. The exploding crime rate was hitting dangerous new levels. Over five hundred people were slain in the DC metropolitan area, including Prince George's in 1993, retaining DC's distinction as the nation's murder capital. I acquired a spray of Mace, which I carried in my purse, and a cellular bag phone that had just been introduced in the market, the prototype of the modern-day mobile phone. The phone was bulky and cumbersome, but it gave me a sense of reassurance, especially while driving back from work at night, in a second-hand car that threatened to break down on long, secluded stretches of the Beltway.

What made the going easier was reconnecting with old friends. Suddenly after all those years of solitary living, I had a community to turn to. We had all enjoyed chatting on 'The World Mirror' so much that we started meeting frequently afterwards. Kaushik and Manish were roommates and I found myself spending all my spare time with them in their cosy two-bedroom apartment, listening to old Kishore Kumar songs while they cooked chicken curry and other *desi* favourites.

As the familiar aroma of *masalas* wafted around us, for the first time in years I felt the ache of homesickness starting to diminish. When Manish and I started dating, it was an extension of the comfort zone I had finally rediscovered after so many years of solitude in America.

"Ash, I'd like you to swing by the police station this afternoon."

I looked up at Dave in surprise. I was busy with an environmental series on the Wetlands of the Chesapeake Bay, a three-part special I was labouring over. Mandy was covering the crime beat this week. Concealing my annoyance, I said, "Can Mandy go?"

"Afraid not, she's out in Suitland, following up on the carjacking murder. She won't be back in time. You will have to go. Take Jim with you."

Once Dave made up his mind, he was unyielding.

"What's the story?" I asked.

Dave looked vague and his answer was just as abstract. "I think it's about our coverage, about the arrest last week."

I arched my eyebrows. If it was regarding coverage, shouldn't the Police Department be speaking to the News Director? "But, I didn't cover that...."

Dave had already turned his back on me and was punching away the evening headlines. The beautiful sight of sunrise over the Chesapeake Bay would have to wait until tomorrow. Jim pulled the van in at the front of the office and we drove down to the police station.

"Any idea why we've been summoned to the police station?" I looked at Jim. He shrugged his shoulders with a non-committal "no idea hon" and began fiddling with the radio stations. Soon he was humming along to *Alive*, a chart-busting Pearl Jam number. When we reached the police station, the receptionist asked us to wait in the foyer. Then she ushered us into the boardroom. "The Police Chief will be here shortly," she smiled at us.

The Police Chief? I was beginning to feel nervous. I looked

Author with Maryland Police Chief

at Jim, who was flipping through a magazine and seemed preoccupied with pictures of motorcycles. Maybe there was a problem with my 'Behind the Badge' series. That's it; it had to be. I had done a three-part special on female police officers in the County Police Force. Clearly, the Police Department had not liked my story and was going to tell me why. I looked around at the plaques and medals adorning the shelves and walls of the wood-panelled room. What a tough job these officers had, I thought. Just then the door opened, and County Police Chief David Mitchell strode in. Jim and I stood up to greet him.

"Ashwini, Jim, how are you both doing?" He shook our hands warmly and enquired about our news day. His eyes twinkled as he spoke to us. Chief Mitchell was highly regarded in Prince

George's County as a man who was successfully fighting for more money for his department and pioneering the community policing initiative in several crime-plagued pockets. Just then, the door opened and his press secretary Mark walked in. He was smiling broadly, as he handed a package to the Chief.

"Ashwini," Chief Mitchell took out a plaque from the package and presented it to me. "This is for the outstanding work you have done for the Police Department these last five years. We heard that you will be leaving PGTV soon and we are indeed very sorry to hear that. We wanted to say thank you."

I was speechless. Jim started laughing and said, "Glad we pulled off this surprise!"

The plaque read: *In grateful appreciation for your outstanding news coverage of the Prince George's County Police Department. Your continuing commitment to fair and unbiased reporting is a credit to your profession. The incorporation of these journalistic values into your coverage of police-related issues has produced an excellent working relationship between the Department and PG Community Television.*

I fought back tears as I posed for a photo next to the Police Chief, holding the plaque proudly in my hands.

As Jim and I drove back to the office, I remained quiet, reflecting on the years gone by and my decision a few weeks ago to leave. PGTV had given me insights into local news reporting in the most powerful country in the world. I discovered that underneath the superpower swagger, small-town life in America was characterised by a simplicity, generosity of spirit and appreciation that welcomed people like me. I held Dave in the highest regard, first as my boss, and later as a friend. He hired me fresh off the boat, willing to take a chance on me, despite my being an accented outsider to local America. My 'foreign-ness' had not deterred him, for which I would always be grateful.

Ultimately it was loneliness, which defined the American way of life, that I was unable to surmount. The silence of the suburbia, which always struck me as deathly still, with cul-de-sacs that looked like handcuffs. I missed home, even though I didn't know where home was. All I knew was, it wasn't *here*. It beckoned from afar, this amorphous abstract of imagery – my parents, sister, grandmothers, uncles, aunts and cousins.

I knew I didn't belong to local news. It was easy to change my accent and my appearance, but I couldn't change my inner self. I knew it was time to leave.

---

I decided to spend a year in India to explore the TV market, which was in its nascent stage, readying for take-off. While there was clarity on the career front, I was much more ambivalent on how to manage a long-distance romance. Luckily, Manish took that decision out of my hands. When the time came for me to leave America, he was by my side, and together we headed to India to seek our parents' blessings. Six months later we were married in Delhi, on a chilly winter evening, in a shower of marigolds and roses, amid beaming family members. My parents were especially relieved that their daughter had finally decided to 'settle down'. If my in-laws felt any unease about my being career-oriented, they did not express it, but rather hoped domesticity would ultimately tame the ogre of ambition.

Manish and I returned to the United States, a land I had been trying so hard to escape from. Boston, with its idyllic Charles

River and brownstone charm became our new home.

No sooner had we been married a year when a job offer tumbled into my world. It happened one afternoon as I sat huddled under my down comforter, enjoying a hot cup of ginger tea, least expecting any upheaval in my life. I stared at the pitch darkness outside my window. It was only three in the afternoon, but it was quintessential Boston winter and it didn't get more miserable than January. The meteorologist on my favourite Weather Channel, which I switched on the minute I woke up, was animatedly describing the severe winter weather predicted over the next few days. The wind chill factor was minus *fifteen* degrees! I shivered at the thought of the Arctic blasts raging outside. I was nursing a cough and cold, and feeling very sorry for myself. The multiple cups of ginger tea were making me terribly homesick for my parents and sister back in India. Just as I reached for the phone to call Aparna, it rang.

Pure telepathy! We sisters just felt it in our bones – the need to speak to each other.

"Hey, guess what, I was just going to call you…." I froze.

It wasn't Aparna at the other end.

"This is Sam Gupta from CNBC in Mumbai. May I speak to Ashwini please?"

I bolted out of bed, forgetting the freezing floor and my cold, and nearly tripped over the phone chord.

"Yes, yes, this is Ashwini." My nose was severely blocked, and I probably sounded like a blubbering idiot.

"Oh hi, Ashwini, how are you? You had sent me your tape some time back. Well, I have some good news. We went through all the resumes and your tape really stood out. We would like to offer you a job in Mumbai."

The winter chill instantly evaporated and I felt sunshine dancing off the hardwood floor. *CNBC was offering me a job?* I can't recall the rest of the conversation, but I am doubly sure I sounded vague and utterly unintelligent, not at all the poised, authoritative anchor-woman they had in mind. But wait a minute, what about *my husband?* During that brief minute of telephonic conversation, I had not only forgotten I had a husband, but also that I was newly married! Mumbai and Boston couldn't be further apart, two opposite ends of the globe. Manish had just found himself a job at a prestigious State Street fund management company and it would be foolhardy to toss it at this stage. It was the classic juggle struggle of a married, career woman.

Manish was determined that I should take this opportunity at all cost. "You've dreamed of this break, you mustn't say no."

"But, it's Mumbai, not Maryland. We won't even be able to see each other often."

No cell phones, no Facebook, no Skype, no FaceTime. And there was no finish line to this job offer. I mean, what if I loved my new job and didn't want to come back to Boston? CNBC, the American media juggernaut, was all poised to enter the Indian market and I was to be part of the freshly-minted team, as their main presenter, at least to begin with. There were ambitious expansion plans, with the channel determined to establish a foothold in one of the world's most exciting emerging economies.

---

I landed in Mumbai in September of 1996.

My identity as a starry-eyed reporter remained unchanged.

The only variable was that I was now a *newly married*, starry-eyed reporter with a husband who was on the far side of the planet.

For the first few months, our studio was the great outdoors, as CNBC did not yet have its own facilities. A cameraman, a soundman and I would drive around in Mumbai's baking heat looking for cinematic backdrops for my on-air intros. I was clocking long hours for our news magazine, 'Inside India', a show I was anchoring solo from the footpaths of Mumbai, on a channel that no one could watch because it aired on an obscure cable platform.

Nevertheless, reporting out of Mumbai was exhilarating.

"I'm doing lots of on-air work," I told my husband on the phone. "It's just that no one gets to see me."

My grandaunt who lived in Mumbai would tell me impatiently, "Why can't I see you on TV? Tell your CNBC people that I can't find your channel anywhere!"

Being new to the market, CNBC, in the early days, was a fairly unknown brand in India. It was competing in a field that had already become crowded with local players including NDTV, STAR-TV, Zee, Sony, and hundreds of small cable operators who were offering viewers a smorgasbord of exciting programming. The media market was exploding, with news channels numbered to be in the 800-range.

Mumbai was a city bursting with news stories that reflected India's new dawn; economic reforms were the buzzword in boardrooms, offices and living rooms. Suddenly India was the poster-kid for emerging economies. American, British, French companies, eager to gain a foothold in the Indian market to bolster poor performances back home, were lining up for contracts, joint ventures and partnerships. It was boom time.

A few months later, CNBC acquired a studio in Prabhadevi, thus ending my era of outdoor-anchoring. The channel hired more people and our team grew. A former investment banker came on board and I now had a new co-anchor. Together we hosted 'Inside India', CNBC's very first business programme that established the channel's presence in a newly liberalising India. The adrenaline rush that came with reporting in India had no parallel. The scale was grand, which we still had not breached, but we knew it was within grasp. Our team was youthful and energetic and we were impatient to get more visibility and recognition for our brand. The local channels had a clear head start over us, with NDTV blazing the way, but we knew it was only a matter of time before CNBC entrenched itself into this media cauldron. We were supported by the winds of change that were sweeping across India. In this frenzied financial capital, with its rotting piles of garbage and high-rises that were beginning to dot the skyline, there was not a single second to pause.

I was struck by how many young people there were around me. It was hard to miss the youthful fervour in Mumbai, it flowed everywhere like a flowering bougainvillea, from the streets, to restaurants to offices, markets and bars.

No wonder then, India's famous demographic dividend, with its burgeoning numbers, was seen as its shining asset. With a whopping two-thirds of the country below the age of thirty-five, India's youth was seen as the tide that would turn India's fortunes, its blueprint for success.

That India was ready to shed years of socialism was music to the ears of financial analysts and bankers, including my husband who was looking after emerging markets in his new company. Private players were being invited to invest in sectors such as insurance, power, telecommunications and banking, freeing them from years of government protection.

Foreign direct investment was rising. Almost every day, I would get calls from PR agencies offering us interviews with multinational companies who were lining up to come to India: from McDonald's to KFC, AIG to Enron, Hyundai and Ford, they were revving up their engines. Indian firms were feeling the heat from the threat of competition; the shake-up was inevitable, one that everyone hoped would result in an increase in both productivity and profitability for local companies, and would be a win-win for both businesses and consumers. India was chugging along at a solid 6 percent growth. The era of the Hindu rate of growth seemed to be permanently behind us.

Along with the demographic dividend, the other word that echoed around me was the 'Great Indian Middle Class', which was being wooed like a beautiful damsel. The magic 300-million number, bigger than the population of America, was alluring. MNCs were vying to introduce their international brands to these educated, globalised consumers who were suave and savvy and more importantly, willing to spend.

It was also the friendly bonhomie of the Indians that made the city a journalist's delight. Their garrulous nature was a boon for soundbites. Most often, it was through casual conversations, whether engaging a corporate professional, a rickshaw driver, a household help or a relative, that led me to those hidden gems of stories that didn't make it to the newspapers. With Bollywood, cricket, the stock market, the underworld, the street vendors, and its limitless layers of energy, the eco-system of Mumbai was intoxicating. It was a city that straddled both poverty and prosperity with equanimity, where dreamers and realists, bound by the immeasurability of aspiration, had an equal shot at success.

It was the thick of monsoons and India's Bollywood queen Madhuri Dixit had agreed to speak to me after repeated calls over several days to her manager. In those days stars typically relied on a secretary to field media requests; they didn't have the PR machinery back then like they do today, circling around them like the rings of Saturn. As our car waded through knee-high water, towards Juhu, my cameraman and I prayed we would make it to our destination, which was anyone's guess while venturing out in the Bombay rains. When we arrived at the bungalow where India's superstar was filming, we stopped in our tracks, bewitched by her megawatt smile that was known to break a million hearts per second. Madhuri Dixit disarmed us with that famous smile, but politely informed us that she could no longer accommodate our request for an interview. In a flash, she was gone.

My interview with India's biggest female star of the nineties would remain an illusion.

---

A few months later, I was sitting in the skylit, stylish CNBC studios in Hong Kong, looking across at the stunning carpet of pointy skyscrapers spread out in front of me. I absorbed the panorama in quiet admiration, marvelling at the Manhattan of the East. As I prepared for my live shot, I couldn't help wonder at the unmistakable similarities between Mumbai and Hong

Kong; both cities, with their spirit of endeavour and imagination, were vanguards of commerce and capitalism. But Hong Kong appeared more vulnerable today, its future misted in uncertainty, as the world geared up for its historic handover to China. In a few days, on July 1, 1997, the British would hand Hong Kong back to China, in exchange for a pledge that the latter would maintain the territory as a commercial hub. A festive mood, tinged by the flicker of an uncertain tomorrow, lingered over the city. In a ceremony marked by many emotions, the Chief Executive of the new Hong Kong government declared the 'one country, two systems' as an endorsement to the city's role as a future capitalist gateway in Asia. There were some protests in the city, but overall the handover was a peaceful, celebratory one.

Anchoring live out of Hong Kong for our audiences back in India was an honour and an epilogue to my chapter with CNBC. The time had come to choose a fork in the road. I took the one that led to my husband, both of us eager to resume our lives in Boston. After all, I'd been away from home for a year and a half. Besides, CNBC India was in the throes of change; there were rumours the channel was planning to tie up with an Indian company, but no one really knew the inside story and how it would impact us. The uncertainty weighed heavily on our team. The time was ripe for me to pack my bags and return home to a more stable and certain future.

CNBC had taken me back to India. Returning to this land after nearly a decade provided me with the assurance that, irrespective of distance and geography, the umbilical link I shared with India could not be severed. In Mumbai, I had moved into the Joshi household. My father's childhood friend, his wife and daughter welcomed me into their fold, showering me with love and affection that only made the homecoming sweeter.

---

For the first time, my reporting career went into suspension mode. Motherhood took over and for two years, I was in a world of diapers, drool and Teletubbies. My TV identity became a heap of VHS and umatic tapes piled up in a big box in my study room.

Two toddlers later, I would be ready to face the studio lights once again.

But this time, in a different country.

Ambassador Vijay Thakur Singh (extreme left) and Vice Admiral Satish Soni (in white) at a reading of Batik Rain, India House, Singapore

## Island in the Rain

**SINGAPORE**
*2000s*

## Singapore

The alarm shrilled, and I leapt out of bed, landing on the floor with a loud thud.

"Ouch."

My husband didn't stir. He had just proven what a solid sleeper he was. Waking up at 4am for the dreaded graveyard shift was becoming torturous. I'd gone to bed at 1am, after trying to soothe my younger son's racking cough. This was the second time in two months Ishan was getting bronchitis. We would have to see an allergy specialist sooner or later; his poor health was a huge worry. But for now, there was no time to think about Ishan's allergies because this was the first day of my 'substitute presenting' shift. The main anchor was on maternity leave and I was stepping in for her for the next three weeks.

Sitting on my bedroom floor, clutching my stinging knee and trying to orient myself to the darkness, while forcing myself to emerge out of the subterranean depths of sleep, I envied the stay-at-home moms. It was moments like this when I badly wished I could swap places with them.

---

I had joined the BBC in the summer of 2003. From running after toddlers in flip flops, to chasing financial analysts for their outlook on key economic events that were shaping the

Asian countries in our backyard, I was suddenly back in the TV studios again – and would spend the next five years working as a reporter and producer for 'Asia Business Report', the channel's flagship business programme in Asia. A new city and two small children could not keep me off the career track for too long. Terrified at the prospect of turning into a 'lady of leisure', a malaise many of my girlfriends had warned me about, I was determined to deep-dive into a job before I got sucked into the eternal polemic that pitted career women against homemakers. "If one spouse is travelling, the other needs to stay put," many of my highly educated girl friends would say over coffee. "Who will look after the children?"

Along with many others, we had come to Singapore in search of a place called home. We flew in, like migratory birds, from various corners of the globe, looking for favourable ecological conditions to raise our young. We met new people, while discovering friends from back home. My husband was delighted to find his old neighbour from Delhi living two floors above us. Anu Raju and her husband Rajan would become the substitute for family, which for many of us, was across the Bay of Bengal.

In our new tropical home, the sun shone permanently bright and pastel rainbows glimmered through the rain. Every morning, birds would begin their chorus while the morning was still dark, impatient for the day to begin. When I peered out of my curtain, a yellow-crested bird would fly in and out of the radiant bougainvillea it seemed to fancy on my balcony. On stormy nights when rain battered the island, I hoped the bird was safe, perched on a broad branch somewhere.

Safe, like the way we felt here, thousands of miles from the land we had left behind. Shortly after the 9/11 attacks, my husband and I, with our two toddlers, left Boston, which had been our home for eight years. We left behind a country writhing in pain and recoiling from the horror of seeing the Twin Towers crumble to dust. We left with fear and shock in our hearts, only to find that terror now had a global footprint.

Our arrival in Singapore in January 2002 coincided with the arrest of thirteen members of the Jemaah Islamiyah, a regional Islamic militant group with links to Al Qaeda, which was planning to bomb several American targets across the city, including the US and British embassies. The arrests were a chilling reminder that even a country like Singapore, reputed for its impeccable record on internal security, could not take its safety for granted. Other countries were not as successful in thwarting terror the way Singapore did. Later that same year, in October 2002, a devastating bomb attack in Bali at a Kuta nightclub left over two hundred people dead, once again bringing the scourge of terror not very far from our doorstep.

---

Like many Americans, we knew very little about Singapore when we arrived here from the States. Most ordinary Americans had either never heard of Singapore, or those who had, thought it was part of greater China. Others remembered it as the country in which American teenager Michael Fay had been caned for vandalism in 1994, a punishment the US media had deemed too excessive for the crime committed. It was remarkable how this singular incident had etched itself so deeply and permanently in the mindscape of Americans, blocking off any other positive information relating to Singapore. Many of our friends in the US could barely conceal their shock that we had voluntarily sought a move to Singapore and chosen to leave the golden gates of America, the ultimate mecca for immigrants.

"Singapore is too sterile," said one friend visiting from the US. "It is authoritarian, there's no place for dissent," said another. "A nanny state," pronounced a friend who had moved here from the UK. "Imagine they ban chewing gum."

But it was multicultural, where Diwali, Hari Raya and Vesak were national holidays, along with Christmas. Where temples and mosques lived side by side, like peaceful neighbours. Where Malay was the national language in a majority-Chinese land. Singapore was predominantly Chinese, yet, as an Indian, I felt so much at home in this country.

The city gave me *carte blanche* to walk the streets freely, without the danger of being brushed, touched or raped. It had become instinctive: to look furtively over my shoulder. That I could now go to work at 4am, enter a building with no one else present but a security guard without my heart thudding with fear, was testament to the high priority Singapore had accorded to keeping its women safe. Years of living alone in America had made me a fearful basket case. But in Singapore, over time, the paranoia began to whittle away, till I was overcome by a childlike giddiness that comes from being free from fear.

"Chinese men don't like Indian women," laughed some of my friends. "So we are safe." While we in the Indian community sometimes made light of it, we were deeply grateful for the cloak of safety draped over our shoulders.

It was every reporter's dream to sit behind the anchor desk and spout gravitas. But to sound intelligent and look glamorous at four in the morning seemed more arduous than scaling Base Camp. At least there you could ditch fashion.

"Your hair looked funny this morning," Aparna who now lived in Hyderabad with her two sons, told me matter-of-factly after the broadcast was over one morning. "What have you done to it?"

"I've rebonded it, so I can jump out of bed and rush to the studio and not a hair will be out of place."

"It looks too ramrod straight. You should go to that hairdresser Ayesha in Lucky Plaza, the one you told me all the Indian ladies go to. But, hair aside, you sounded good; great, in fact," she added.

The upside of the morning shift was that I was home by 2pm. While that sounded good in theory, I realised very quickly that the frenetic pace of the morning broadcasts reduced me to a vegetable for the rest of the day. Doctor's visits and allergy specialists quickly plummeted down the priority list; sleep took top billing. Once again, it was grandparents to the rescue. My parents were living in Singapore, thanks to my father's assignment at a local think tank. His post-retirement job had brought them close to me, just when I needed them the most.

"Mom, please can you take Ishan to the doctor? I don't think the medicines he gave are working, he seems worse."

"Ashwini, I was supposed to go with your father to meet Professor Kim about my book...."

"I'm on earlies all of this week, I *can't*. Please can you take him?"

"Ok, ok, I'll take him tomorrow morning," said Mom. "Also, what have you done to your *hair*?"

There was no escaping a 'two-way' with London. While presenting made my stomach churn, a live back-and-forth with an anchor sitting in London made me feel like I was being led to the abattoir. The day of my grand debut dawned sunny and bright.

"Don't read too fast, slow down a bit. You're always in a hurry, remember to pause," warned my husband.

"Good luck, I'm sure you'll do great," said Anu.

"Please don't wear that green suit again," joked her husband Rajan, the last person I had imagined would notice my sartorial choice. I vowed to go shopping that weekend for business suits.

Armed with these edicts, I made my way to the studio, relieved that it was Larry, my favourite producer, who was in charge of the show. His ability to maintain sangfroid in the midst of newsroom tumult helped put everyone at ease. I was soon seated at the anchor desk, lapel mike clipped on to my suit, and my hair sprayed into submission. I quickly read through my scripts and checked that the teleprompter was set to the first story, even as my heart began to pound. I had enough practice with the prompter now, how much pressure to apply on the foot pedal so it moved along at a speed that was comfortable.

"Don't worry Ash, you'll be fine," Larry gave me a thumbs-up, as he closed the studio door and went back to the control room.

I was alone.

I adjusted my jacket and hair, and did a mike test, "Testing, testing, voice check." Two minutes to air.

"We've got Jack on. Ash, he wants to speak to you, I'm putting him through."

Jack was the London anchor, by far the best in the business – crisp, charming and utterly flawless. Of all the anchors, why did it have to be *him*, today?

"Hi Ashwini, good to have you doing the live with me today. So, are we starting off with Samsung's results?"

"Yes, that's right, Samsung followed by Thai elections."

"I've got two questions on the elections, very straightforward. It's all looking good. Good luck, and I'll see you in a bit."

My hands felt moist and clammy. And my throat felt dry. What if I coughed in the middle, or even worse, got the hiccups? We were 30 seconds to air.

3-2-1, the red light on the camera came on.

"Good morning, I am Jack Carrington in London."

"And I'm Ashwini Devare in Singapore."

I felt surprisingly calm. I could see the monitor from the corner of my eye; the two of us were up on screen in our respective boxes. We got through the first story on the Samsung results without a hitch. I was satisfied with my pace, while simultaneously turning the scripts. We moved on to the recently concluded Thai elections and Jack asked me what the outcome was. I ad-libbed the first few lines and turned to the prompter for the rest of the story. To my horror, I saw the earlier Samsung story was still up, in big bold font. Where was the Thai story? Was the prompter STUCK? *Were prompters allowed to get stuck during live broadcasts?* I pushed the foot pedal down hard, but the prompter remained frozen solid. I lost all my composure and began to flub.

"Er, the Thai elections, er, took place this morning, er...." I started flipping through the scripts, which made matters worse, because in my panic I jumbled the order. I was alone in a vast wilderness of live television. The shock in the control room was palpable. Could the anchor desk please open up and swallow me? I could do the Sita act and disappear into the bowels of this earth forever. Luckily Jack – and God bless the man – jumped in with his velvet voice. "The Thai elections are seen as a turning point, with the Red Shirts winning…" As Jack started ad-libbing, the camera zoomed to him, and the live hit ended with his goodbye. Said Priscilla, my wonderful producer friend who never minced a single word, "Not exactly the best debut."

I sat in the studio, not wanting to walk out and face the newsroom. The editor walked in, along with Larry, who was grinning. "Don't worry, Ash, it was literally a few seconds before we went to Jack. Not as bad as you think." This is why I loved Larry.

"I'm sorry. It was a disaster." I wanted to cry. Crying would make me look like a weak reporter. Or maybe it might just redeem me.

"It wasn't ideal," said the editor. "But as Larry said, we guessed the prompter had frozen and immediately went to Jack. Lesson learned is you need to practise ad-libbing. Presenters must never rely on the prompter."

I survived and luckily kept my job.

---

"Ash, can you do the day shift on Monday?" I stared blankly at Mark, our new editor from London.

I had promised to take Aman and Ishan to the bookstore on

Monday, an outing we had been planning ever since the new Percy Jackson book came out a week ago. Going to Kinokuniya on Orchard Road was an excursion the kids looked forward to with great excitement. The day shift meant I wouldn't get home till late in the evening.

"Uh, sure," I found myself saying. It was nearing 7pm. It was nice and quiet in the office; just the sound of typing and the background hum of the TV monitor. The sky was darkening. Aman and Ishan were back from school and had a tennis lesson. If it didn't rain, I'd have to book a cab for my helper, who was on standby to take them for their class.

But Mark had other plans.

"So what's our line-up for the first show on Monday?" He came around my desk, glancing over my running order. I dreaded that question, especially when it came towards the end of the Friday shift. I had spent all afternoon confirming two live guests for the programme, but hadn't managed to find a third person.

"There's a potentially explosive story that's just coming off the wires, we might have to find a live guest on that," Mark was saying.

Find a *live* guest at 7pm on a Friday? Markets in Australia and Japan were already closed and Singapore had shut a while ago. Besides, everyone had packed up and gone home. What new story was Mark talking about?

"Well," I mustered my most convincing tone and began, "we usually don't book guests on Friday evening for a Monday morning show because things will change over the weekend, the story's definitely going to get old by then."

It began to rain, loud pitter-pats hitting the glass windows.

"Sorry, who did you say you've got for the early show?" Mark was poring through the wires and hadn't listened to a word of what I'd said. He was the archetypal New Editor On the March.

"Yong from Powernomics, talking about the ASEAN-China FTA," I said, in my most enthusiastic voice. "He's going to discuss tariff cuts and other key bits of the agreement as well as...."

"Drop Yong. We need a financial guy, a banker. We have to hurry."

*Say what?* My heart started pumping. I'd spent half the morning chasing Yong who had finally agreed to do the show after much coaxing and now Mark wanted me to ditch him? I quickly scanned through the wires for this breaking story Mark was being so tight-lipped about. My mobile started ringing and I knew it was my helper waiting for instructions on whether to go for the tennis lesson.

"Something tells me this weekend is going to be huge," said Mark. He started making some calls.

"Hi, yes, this is Mark here," he sat up straight. "Yes, yes, tell me. Really? Seriously? Man, that's crazy." It was the first time I'd seen Mark so tense. He put the phone down and sat still for a few seconds. Then he turned to me and said, "That was my friend from New York, the one who got fired from Lehman last week. There's mayhem on Wall Street."

It was time to put on our seat belts; we were in for a very bumpy ride.

The rain was coming down in sheets, even as a far more powerful storm was about to pummel Asia. The phones started ringing furiously, simultaneously. My phone beeped. My banker husband was freaking out. China was down, no it couldn't be, down 30 percent and still falling! A bloodbath was about to decimate the markets.

"Asia is going to be impacted pretty badly," said Mark. "Sovereign wealth funds in the region have wide exposure to toxic assets in the US. They're likely to face huge losses." Mark was pacing up and down the newsroom, clicking his pen furiously.

Following the 1998 financial crisis which shattered Asian economies, the region had rebounded, emerging markets had strengthened their fundamentals and growth prospects were strong. The theory of Asia 'decoupling' from the US was becoming a popular theme among economists who enthusiastically supported the idea that the emerging world should reduce its dependency on the West. Thailand and Indonesia that had been so badly buffeted in '98 were looking robust. It didn't seem fair that a subprime mortgage crisis in suburban USA should affect Asia.

Mark glanced across at me. "London wants a live cut-in, in an hour. We need someone *ASAP*." Mark picked up the phone and started making calls.

It was going to be a very long night. It seemed just as bad for my husband who was worried that his entire bank would collapse, taking all of us down with it. The grandparents had been summoned. My selfless, adorable parents who were permanently on call and had to step in every time I abandoned the children, which was pretty much all the time these days. On breaking news nights like this, there was no time to think about your *other* life. My husband wasn't going home anytime soon either. My sons were at home, happily doing everything they weren't supposed to do, watching TV and playing Nintendo.

"They've been on it for three hours?" I said to my mother, horrified. "Can you *please* get them off the gadgets!"

I spoke in a low tone to my mother who was complaining that the boys weren't listening to her. One eye on the TV monitor waiting for updates, the other half of my brain could hear the kids shouting in the background.

"Why's Aman crying?"

"Ishan snatched his book. Ashwini what time are you coming home?"

"Mom, I don't know," I gritted my teeth. Mothers never got the urgency of the situation sometimes. "I can't talk, it's a huge story."

"But what about your dinner? Have you eaten something?"

"Mom, I really have to go, bye…" Ugh.

"Ash, have you found anyone?"

I hoped Mark hadn't heard my back and forth with my mother. I called all our usual suspects, our regular finance gurus. No one was taking my calls. I began to panic.

Every call we made dead-ended. It was 7:45pm. I knew Mark was not going to tell his bosses in London he hadn't been able to find them a live guest; that would be instant death. This was the time for me to tap the Indian community, my reliable constituency. Heck, why do we have so many Diwali parties and Holi shebangs? The networking is par excellence. We had a banker friend whom we had never tested on air. He was a good friend, think-he-has-a-crush-on-me-but-not-sure kind of guy. The time had come to call him.

"Shyam, hi, it's Ashwini. Sorry are you driving? Oh, you are still in the office? Listen, I need a huge favour! Please can you do a live interview for us, in our studio? On Lehman and the impact on Asia. Now, I mean, in the studio, yes, in about half an hour's time."

Please God please, Shyam say yes, say yes. He was hesitating; I jumped in, desperate. "It'll just take 5 minutes, it's a live broadcast, so you will be done really fast. It will be seen in India too, of course, do you think you could swing by our office, please?" I'm sure Shyam could sense the panic in my voice. Mark was looking expectantly at me, hoping for this Shyam friend of Ash's to come through.

"Ok, ok, just for you, Ashwini. *Tere liye kucch bhi.*"

"He said yes!"

"Thank God," said Mark, leaning back in his chair with his hands clasping his face. "Alright everybody, quick, let's get going, Lee get the studio ready. Myra get the cameras out. Live shot with London!" Mark ordered, running around the office. "Ash, you're a lifesaver."

The monsoon wasn't weakening anytime soon, heavy rain pummelled the windows. Inside the studio, it was our biggest story yet; we were on top of it and Shyam was delivering his best soundbite, his most articulate analysis. I almost fell in love with Shyam at that moment. The storm that began that night would go on for months, obliterating Asian stock markets, the financial world, pulverising businesses, reducing CEOs to ground zero and thousands of people would lose their jobs. Mark and I shared the adrenaline rush of reporting on a story that we would never forget. It was a bond that remained till the end of his two-year stint. Today I consider him as one of my best editors and a solid friend.

---

A few weeks later, I was at the mall with my sons. As usual, Ishan was focused on what he should, could, or would buy at Toys"R"Us. Even at the age of eight, Ishan was an ace negotiator who routinely managed to get the rest of the family to capitulate to his demands. He started to convince his brother on what he thought Aman should buy. Aman became angry and burst out, "Don't you know there's recession? It's a financial crisis!"

"What's that?" said Ishan stubbornly, pulling my hand in the direction of the toy store. "I don't care."

"You should!" cried Aman. "We can't spend that much now. Banks don't have money. Mommy, how long is the recession?" Aman, the quiet worrier, looked very troubled. "Maybe I should stop having school lunch because there's recession."

"Aman, times may not be good right now, but believe me, you don't need to stop buying school lunch. We're fine," I patted his head, as I firmly walked them away from the store and out of the mall.

The financial storm left much debris in its wake. Many of our friends lost jobs, others closed shop overnight and relocated, never to return. Through the churning and upheavals in our new island-home, solid bonds of friendships had emerged, nurtured over the many years of living side by side in a community we could turn to in times of need, an itinerant group of people with similar interests, hopes and aspirations. We had tackled the initial challenges of adjusting to a new land, helping one another with playschools for our children or simply sending one another home-cooked meals. When the scourge of Sars hit, we had hunkered in, together, providing information and assistance to one another, as the deadly pneumonia-like virus claimed thirty-three lives and infected over two hundred in the city-state. With the city virtually shut down, we had turned to each other for comfort, and taken collective pride in Singapore's fight against Sars, which was seen as a tour de force, and its handling of the crisis won it plaudits around the world.

---

We had escaped Sars, but we could not escape the next wave of virus that came sweeping across Asia. I got home from work one afternoon to find Aman curled up on the sofa, fast asleep. This in itself was unusual, since my older son, a poor sleeper, rarely napped. Aman had come home from school shivering and feverish. The next morning the doctor ran a blood test and to our horror, it turned out he had Influenza A (H1N1), also known as swine flu.

"Will he be alright?" I whispered to the doctor, trying to quell the wave of anxiety that was rising from my stomach up to my throat.

"Start the Tamiflu immediately," said the doctor. I had heard rumours that there could be a shortage of Tamiflu in Singapore; the antiviral drug used in the treatment of H1N1, even though the government had announced it was increasing its stockpile of the vaccine.

"Aman, are you ok?" I asked my son several times a day, as I placed cool strips on his burning forehead. The deadly swine flu was spreading rapidly around the world. Once again, it was a virulent strain of influenza with no precedent, one that had not been identified as a cause of infections in the past. Meanwhile, there was a growing concern in the medical community that swine flu could become resistant to Tamiflu and therefore would be more difficult to treat.

When Aman recovered and I returned to work, I struggled to focus on the day-to-day grind of daily news. A month later my younger son was hospitalised for salmonella, an illness I never dreamed could afflict anyone in this squeaky-clean city. Juggling children who were far sicklier than their peers with a high-octane job was taking its toll. At thirty-eight, I was beginning to feel like a dinosaur. While the news business was getting younger, especially in Asia, the forties were creeping up on me. It was time for a re-evaluation of priorities.

Aman's swine flu episode, which felt like a battle cry, convinced me that perhaps this was the time to build up their immune systems rather than my CV. After five years of working for the BBC, I decided to hand in the mike and bid adieu to a thirteen-year career in broadcast news.

A few days before I left the BBC, I had coffee with my producer friend Priscilla, who had been working in television news for more than twenty years.

"How do you burn out at forty?" I asked her. "I mean, this is the beginning, yet it feels like the end."

"I'm burnt out too," confided Priscilla. "I'm thinking of doing other things, I mean there *is* a world out there apart from television." I stared at her open-mouthed. Priscilla was the best television producer in the business. I couldn't imagine her doing anything else.

A few weeks later, she resigned.

---

I was back to wearing flip-flops again, except now I wasn't chasing my kids across the sand pit anymore. In those five years, while I'd been running around getting soundbites, my children had grown up.

"I need a head-torch," said Ishan, reading through a list his teacher had sent home. "It's for night kayaking."

"Just borrow one from your friend," I said. We were packing for Ishan's field trip to Tioman Island, which had a mile-long checklist of items that needed to be purchased.

"What the hell, the teacher told us we have to have our own head-torch. It's very important!"

I decided to ignore his language, which was becoming too colourful for my liking.

"I looked in all the camping stores, they didn't have any," I said, trying not to sound defensive. I had spent the entire afternoon going to various camping stores, annoyed at the school for making parents run around as if they had nothing better to do. Most of the stores had run out of head-torches.

"You didn't go to the right shop," said Ishan accusingly.

"Well maybe you should have come with me. Am I expected to run around doing all your errands?" I yelled back.

From being answerable to no one, I was now accountable to my pre-teens. It felt surreal.

Alpha moms, I discovered, were just as formidable as alpha career women, if not more. They juggled their households and social lives with a mastery that was admirable; I found myself utterly at a loss around them.

The role of stay-at-home-mom was taking a lot more time to adjust to than I'd anticipated. Suddenly I was thrust into the world of school curricula, field trips and parent-teacher meetings that I felt inadequately equipped to handle. While my friends would wade through the maze of academic acronyms with consummate artistry, I found myself floundering. Years of following business trends and geopolitical developments in Southeast Asia were now being replaced with comparative analysis between IB, IGCSE, 'A' levels and the American AP systems, Trinity versus ABRSM and GCs (Global Concerns), a foundation for the philanthropy platform espoused by IB schools.

It would take some time for me to acknowledge that I had officially become a helicopter parent, after denying it for so long. I now had newfound respect for homemaker-moms who had eased into this role gracefully while I still battled questions of identity in my head.

---

The aura of being a broadcast journalist that had subsumed me for a large part of my adult life dimmed once the cameras were switched off. I no longer felt the over-arching desire to see myself on television, which had powered me when I first joined the industry.

The accent demon had reared its ugly head through my career and demolished my self-esteem. In America, I didn't sound American enough for mainstream TV. In India, I sounded too American for prime time TV; at the BBC I sounded too American. I waded in no man's land for years.

That I had finally vanquished the accent nemesis was hugely emancipating. I remember once an editor from London emailed me after she saw one of my on-air reports. She pointed out that she did not like how I had pronounced 'leisure' the American way, as *lee-sure*. "The English way is *lay-sure*," she said. After that, every time I walked into the audio booth to record my voice-over, I would rehearse the script several times to ensure no American bits were leaking into my narration.

Another time I heard from Dr Prannoy Roy, the founder of NDTV, one of India's leading TV channels. I had worked with NDTV briefly in the mid-nineties, after I'd quit working for PGTV in Maryland. Dr Roy happened to see one of my on-air reports from Singapore. "Whatever happened to your American accent?" he asked good-humouredly.

Now, finally, after all these years I can speak in my very own hybrid accent over which I have full ownership.

---

As the years scrolled by, my children became teenagers, and the Singapore skyline continued to change, glittering jewels in a velvet sky. The boats bobbed along the Singapore River, against the backdrop of the magnificent Marina Bay Sands arched across the sunset sky. Audacious and stylish, the spectacular 55-storeyed architectural marvel dazzled the city's horizon. As it soared into the clouds, so did Singapore, its economy fighting back to shake off the effects of the financial crisis. Moshe Safdie's magical creation was just the shot in the arm the city-state needed as visitors poured in, in droves from all around Asia, bringing in millions of tourist dollars.

Singapore bloomed in a multitude of colours.

---

A decade had flashed by. Another had begun. My sister too had her own family now, two boys just like mine. When we met, every few months, we would giggle like we used to and the years would vanish, taking us right back to the pomelo tree in our garden in Rangoon. We chuckled over her acronym 'PTDP' and the letter she had written to my father in Seoul, complaining about my mother's and my compulsive spending habits. We recalled the time the four of us had stood in front of the Berlin Wall, chipping away at it till we had secured a piece of history tightly in our fists.

Our lives had been ruled by the words, *where next:* simple, innocuous words that had tormented us. The jitters would begin a year and a half after settling into a new country, as we fretted over what penance lay ahead. That the Ministry of External Affairs in Delhi, with a single stroke of a pen, not unlike British officer Cyril Radcliffe who drew the line separating India and Pakistan, would sign off on our destinies every three years, would be a source of great angst for us both. We would brace ourselves to being flung from great heights of luxury into pits of penury. When we jumped, we held hands to break the fall, to soften our landing.

Aparna is still frugal and wise, just like she used to be when she was eight years old. There is so much to share, but never enough time to linger over the years gone by. The pressures of day to day prevail: children, husbands, parents, friends – all part of that giant cycle of life that continues to rotate. We feel thankful for our nomadic life, which sealed us like glue, keeping our closeness intact, despite the vagaries and the vicissitudes that came our way.

When the four of us meet, our parents and us, the dining table once again becomes the edifice for our discussions, which are just as vigorous, but the topics of conversation have changed somewhat. Grandchildren and their evolving personalities have taken centre stage, their mastery over technology and their confidence a source of great pride for my parents. As grandparents, they long for the teenagers' attention and are grateful for just a few moments with them in a day. Even that is enough to give them immense joy in a life that is becoming increasingly lonely.

Time feels more fragile now, much more so than it ever did. There is a pressing desire to hurry, to write, and *do*.

---

*Batik Rain* had been lurking in my head for many years, like a cloud heavy with rain. The characters in my short stories were becoming real to me with each passing day. Then the cloudburst happened and the stories came pouring down. It was the end of one chapter, but the beginning of another, which would allow me to express myself in sentences, rather than in soundbites.

It felt as if the sky was flooding the Earth. A monsoon downpour of an intensity not seen in years was lashing the city on the very evening of my book launch at the Singapore Writers Festival. The deluge wreaked havoc on the Friday evening rush hour, creating gridlock in the busy Orchard area. As sheets of rain pelted around us, I waited anxiously inside the big white tent that had been allocated for my event, wondering if anyone would turn up. As the rain hammered down, I prayed fervently that the tent would hold up.

"Let's delay the start of the programme by fifteen minutes," the organiser suggested. I nodded gratefully, looking out at the rows of empty seats. The title of my book, *Batik Rain*, seemed rather too fitting for the occasion. My husband and sons were standing in the rain, ushering those who might be lost. A trickle of people walked into the tent, with wet hair and soaked shoes, holding their dripping umbrellas. As they settled into their seats, the roar of the rain suddenly quietened, and raindrops pattered about the tent, suggesting the storm might be past. I heaved a sigh of relief, even as I began to feel butterflies in my tummy.

The moderator and I took our positions on stage, as more people walked in. By the time we started the programme, the tent, with a capacity of a hundred and fifty, was full. To my shock, there were quite a few people standing at the back. That there were so many familiar faces in the crowd, friends who had taken the effort to be here on this rain-drenched evening, to support my momentous occasion was overwhelming. I felt dangerously close to tears. When my moderator asked me, "Tell us about your influences, what inspired you?" it was inconceivable that the answer could be far from *here*, right now, in this very tent, in this very town, under the drizzling stars and inkiness of the night, the magic of the familiar embracing us, as we huddled, safe, dry, in the comfort of the present.

---

We are who we are.

Shaped by the varied influences we encounter through our lives. The story our grandmothers told us, the whiff of our mother's sari, a quiet moment shared with a father, a sister, a brother, a friend, a teacher. They have played a part in making us whole. These influences are intrinsic to us all, to me, as they hovered and seeped into my consciousness.

"I've never seen so many people at a book launch," one of the SWF organisers would tell me later. "Who were all those people?"

"My extended family," I said. "Each one of them in the room was special, with whom I share a connection."

It is easy to crash-land back to earth from stratospheric musings when you have teenagers in the house. The 'me' moment of acquiring a 'published author status' was remarkably brief in the face of bigger calamities like break-ups, spider sightings and lost socks. My young men weren't aware that path-breaking, 'epochal' moments were redefining my life and that I was poised for my breakout moment, or perhaps, was it more like a mid-life crisis.

"Mom, no one reads books anymore," said Ishan, as he scrolled through the shots he was going to use in his short film. Ishan's passion for filmmaking was growing in quantum leaps.

"You can't make good films if you don't read," I retorted.

"Mom, you have to do videos, trust me. Why don't you make a show about journalism or tutorials or something? I'll upload them for you on YouTube."

"Why would I do that?"

"See, the problem with you is that you just don't want to reinvent yourself. Seriously, if you did this journalist tutorial kind of videos, you'd get thousands of views. Like *thousands*."

"And what will I do with views?"

"Forget it, Mom," said Ishan. Through our entire conversation, Ishan hadn't looked up from his screen; we may as well have been speaking to each other on the phone. "Mom, don't get me wrong, I'm really proud you wrote a book," he said, finally looking up.

"And who knows, maybe I can make a film on one of your short stories some day. That way people will actually read your book."

That was undisputedly the best compliment I could have asked for from my fourteen-year-old.

I'm not sure when my toddlers morphed into argumentative teenagers.

My mind flits back to sixteen years ago.

Two little boys dug into the sand with their chubby hands and pulled out a fistful. Foreheads furrowed in deep concentration, sweat clinging to their backs, they squatted side by side on the beach, as afternoon changed to evening.

"Let's build a castle," said Ishan, in his hoarse voice.

"I want to build a dinosaur," Aman said in his softer, gentle voice.

"It's easier to build a castle," argued Ishan, always one to convince his brother, and the two started building the ramparts of the castle, losing track of time as they focused on the task in front of them. Suddenly Ishan got up and started running towards the water. "I want to swim!"

Aman looked up in alarm and tried to stop him. "It's dangerous, stop!" Aman burst into tears, terrified that he was going to lose his brother to the waves.

"Don't worry, I've got him," said their Dad, picking his son up and lifting him high into the air, making him squeal with laughter. "You are the naughty one, our little dragon boy."

"But you, Aman, you are our favourite one," I said, giving my older son a hug.

These are among many snapshots of the brothers, their names hyphenated, but never separate, their togetherness an unalterable status quo of their childhood. One quiet, the other garrulous; one a dreamer, the other a pragmatist, their individualism inscribed into their universe even before they turned six. One took the lead, the other followed, but mostly they remained side by side, always knowing they had each other.

The stability that had been missing in my childhood became theirs.

---

As a television reporter, my life was about moving on to the next story. Deadlines meant there was no time for reflection. Even catastrophic, life-altering events were squeezed into two-minute packages. Now, as a spectator to news, I had time to pause and absorb the historic developments around me.

When Lee Kuan Yew, the founding father of Singapore, the city-state's most famous brand name around the world, passed away, his death caused shock and disbelief across the island. It was hard to visualise a Singapore without Lee Kuan Yew. His presence was all around us, even though he had long retired from public life. As Anu Raju and I joined the serpentine queue that snaked its way around the Padang towards Parliament House, where his body lay in state, we were aware of being part of a watershed moment in the history of the city-state. The air was heavy with sadness, the passing of an era. When dawn streaked the sky, it felt as if the entire population of Singapore had spilled into the streets to mourn the passing of the man known simply as LKY.

It came as no surprise that the Americans and North Koreans chose Singapore to host the landmark summit between Presidents Kim Jong-un and Donald Trump. The two leaders came, conquered and departed in one seamless, theatrical flourish leaving the 3,000-odd media assembled in Singapore to catch their breath from a meeting that felt more like a spectacle than a serious political event.

To imbibe some of the history unfolding in our backyard, my good friend Parul and I walked along Tanglin Road where President Kim Jong-un was staying. We came upon a media hullabaloo: an armada of reporters waiting outside the hotel, TV cameras pointed at the entrance for a glimpse of the reclusive Kim.

"I can't believe I belonged to that fraternity once," I said, looking at the photographers hustling to get the right shots. "It feels like such a long time ago."

"Do you miss it?" asked Parul.

I looked at the reporters, standing in the hot sun, some of them getting ready for their live shots. "No," I said. "Surprisingly, I don't." It was an epiphany of sorts, my very own moment of reckoning, that I had finally achieved closure to the television chapter of my life.

My mind wandered back to a dreary winter afternoon thirty years ago, when my family and I visited the small village of Panmunjom, located in the demilitarised zone (DMZ), the no-man's land, which separates North Korea from the South. The heavily fortified, four-kilometre stretch of DMZ was a cold and forbidding place, where the air felt heavy with the threat of war. We stood there, on the 'safe' side of the demarcation line, which was drawn when the Korean War ended in 1953. My sister and I watched the soldiers nervously, afraid to cough or sneeze lest any noise should disturb their concentration. It was on our drive back home that we would become acutely aware that we were only 50 kilometres from the border that divided the two countries. We understood then, for the first time, the depth of South Korean vulnerability and the unease they felt about their enemy up North.

---

While I lost myself in the labyrinth of parenthood and the preoccupations of modern life, there was a lingering awareness that my parents too were ageing, their fragility becoming more apparent with every passing year. That they too are like children now, who need ample nurturing. When my sister and I visit my parents' home in Delhi, my father's favourite ritual is to walk his daughters around their small apartment bursting with memorabilia, with commentary that magically takes us back in time. A ballerina, my mother's first purchase in Moscow; a cut glass bowl she got in Washington from collecting grocery vouchers; an antique Chosun-dynasty dowry chest acquired in Seoul; several of my Enid Blyton books, musty and frayed, lining the bookshelf. And of course, there's my mother's famous *tanpura*, which went along with her in her trousseau when she got married. It continues to take pride of place in her bedroom, storing in its hollow many a story from distant lands, as it travelled from place to place with us. My mother's voice has aged, but the *tanpura* is as melodious as ever, always in sync with the rhythm of their lives.

---

I live amid a cluster of buildings in a leafy complex. The continuity of this single space, which has dominated my existence since I came to Singapore, is a sharp contrast to the cross-continental drifts I experienced earlier in life. After years of trying to 'fit in' in the West, it was here, on this lush island, with its coconut and banana trees that I found the right soil conditions to evolve.

In this gated greenhouse, neighbours became friends and close friends became family. I met others who, like me, were at the crossroads; they too found their moorings and anchored into their new home. In this borderless world, we are bound together by a common diasporic weave, facing similar challenges of displacement and integration. Through the drifting and the soul-searching has come a resilience to overcome the odds. Despite being more inter-connected than ever before, there's a growing isolation and a greater need to reach out to one another. In this comfort zone that we have created, we find ways to share and appreciate one another.

Kishore Kumar's evergreen *musafir hoon yaaron* plays softly in the background. We sink into the sofas, in the familiar comfort of Anu and Nilesh's home, where we spend many an evening along with the Sharmas, listening to old Hindi songs, chatting about our college-bound children, our empty nests, our jobs, cricket, Bollywood, our present and our future. Each time we meet, it is a celebration of friendship, a savouring of the moment before it slips into the past. Who knows where we will all be tomorrow? As each one of us crosses the forties threshold and embraces the fifties, we are aware, more than ever before, of our surroundings. As always we ponder over the ephemeral shape of home. India, a country that we all left behind, beckons from afar. Some return, others like us have embraced new environs: this island that has brought us together.

Today this city is changing just as we are. Amid the modernity, I find myself looking for solace in spaces that are reposeful and spiritual.

The sun was so harsh it hurt my eyes. I tried to seek refuge in the shadow of a tree, but its canopy was too sparse to provide any shelter. I walked past a row of offices, the sun following me purposefully, as it bounced off the concrete. Hidden amid grey buildings, a red-pillared door stood slightly ajar, revealing a dim, cavernous interior of a Buddhist temple. I stepped inside and the scent of incense swirled around me, taking me instantly back to the monastery in the mountains of Seoul that I had visited with Shinjin so many years ago.

As I stood there, an old lady appeared from inside the depths of the temple, and looked at me inquiringly.

"Can I pray here?" I asked, hesitating, an intruder in a sacred space. She nodded her head towards the incense sticks and raised three gnarled fingers. Gratefully, I lit the sticks and knelt down on the floor. The world outside ceased to exist; the physicality of the present was overpowering. I am not sure how long I knelt there, but it must have been for quite some time, because the lady appeared again and this time she gave me a toothless smile.

---

The nomadic journey that began fifty years ago has run its course, a river merging into the sea. In the circle of this rainy island, where seasons blur and the sun shines so bright after a thunderous shower, my wandering past has yielded to a permanence that had eluded me most of my life.

In this newfound stability, I have found reassurance.

Entering the fifties is like listening to Indian classical music in reverse. While youth represented the hectic *taans*, the thirties and forties were the medium-tempo *dhrut*, with fifty the beginning of *vilambit*, a measured and deliberate rhythm that can only be imbibed through spiritual concentration.

    I believed turning fifty was asymptotic, that it would elude me, like infinity. I was lost at fifteen, trapped in a multitude of identities. For too long I tampered with my identity to suit the habitat I was in, becoming a chameleon so I wouldn't stick out. At fifty, the ritualised longing for belonging that marked the early years has receded. I'm no longer a prisoner to the imbroglio of complexities that entangled me. Surrounded by my flowering bougainvilleas, my mind is fertile and free. Like Jonathan Livingston Seagull, I just want to glide over the shimmering sea.

---

Luminous lanterns sway in the festive alleyways. The streets are dressed in finery, like an Indian bride, in red and gold. Kumquat trees, laden with orange-like fruit, line the streets. As evening falls, a serpentine dragon roars over the rooftops, its long golden shadow illuminating the decorated streets below. Two small boys crouch in fear. They are afraid to look up, yet they can't avert their eyes from this powerful magical creature with its fiery mouth and electric red eyes that seem to follow them.

    "Is that a monster?" asks Ishan, hiding behind me.

"Will it chase us?" asks Aman, in a whisper. He pulls his younger brother towards him, instinctively protective. Two brothers, so close in age, they could be twins.

"No, my dear, it's not a monster, it's a dragon," I said. "Don't be afraid, it won't hurt you."

"Am I a dragon?" asks Ishan, craning his neck to look at the twisting creature, scattering mists of red and gold into the air.

"Yes, indeed you are, you are a Golden Dragon," their father tells Ishan.

"Maybe it knows you were born in the year of the dragon," Aman tells his brother, suddenly feeling less afraid. "Maybe it wants to say hello."

"Yes, it wants to shower us with blessings, it is very auspicious," their father says.

The flying serpent seemed to smile down at us from its royal perch, as it bobbed its head up and down, swishing its glorious tail and gusting balls of fire into the moonless night.

To be born in the year of the Golden Dragon is a supreme honour, I was told by a wizened old woman in the heart of the Forbidden City during a visit to Beijing, while her trembling hands calligraphed my son's name onto a polished marble egg. He will be bold and daring, he will conquer the world, she said in hushed reverence. I held the smooth egg, my fingers sliding over the tiny red squiggle she had imprinted on its surface.

---

The moon hangs low in a cloudy sky, illuminating the landscape below in an ethereal glow. The topography changes as it plays hide-and-seek; foreign lands loom out of misty shores, offering a tantalising glimpse of what they conceal within.

Flashbacks come frequently, nostalgic fragments of moments and places. A small girl and boy running through a Himalayan wood, arms full of rhododendrons; the golden silhouette of the Shwedagon Pagoda blurring into the Merlion as it gazes out at the red-lantern boats in the water; soldiers in camouflage taking notes on the Meiji Rule in a history class merge with two little children staring transfixed at a row of ants making their way over a grassy mound.

The moon drifts out of the clouds as if it too wants to catch a glimpse of the tableau I am drawn to. The luminosity fades, and as the picture starts to evaporate, I am flooded by a deep, inexplicable sense of both fulfillment and loss. Perhaps this is what the void is, the chasm where moonbeams cannot reach. The hubris of youth has parted, like water behind a racing motorboat. Just then, the moon disappears, plunging the landscape into pitch darkness.

---

As individuals in a fusion world, we are all drifting.

Like boats, bobbing up and down, looking for the shoreline, sometimes it's elusive, other times so close.

You think you are home. But is it really your home? Will it accept you? Will it hug you back? After all, you abandoned it, didn't think you would ever come back. Perhaps, like a mother, who unconditionally embraces her child, you expect the same of your country.

## Acknowledgements

I am grateful to the team at Marshall Cavendish for believing in this book. I would especially like to thank Anita Teo for her professional guidance and patient supervision of the book from start to finish. My editor Violet Phoon's meticulous editing of the manuscript and her helpful suggestions were invaluable.

My gratitude also goes to Mr K Kesavapany for his encouragement of all my projects. I would like to acknowledge the entire IFS family, a community I grew up with, for their support.

I am indebted to my family for always being there for me. Manish, Aman and Ishan, the lively, opinionated men in my life, you are the pillars upon which I lean, my inspiration.

And finally, I remain forever grateful to my parents and my sister Aparna, all of them authors, who continue to inspire me to do better. Without all those animated discussions, this book would not have come to life. Mom and Dad, thank you for holding us together through our rollercoaster ride and for all the safe landings.

## About the Author

Ashwini Devare is a journalist and author. She has worked for BBC's Asia Business Report and CNBC Asia. Her first book *Batik Rain* (2014) received critical acclaim and was longlisted for the Frank O'Connor Short Story Award. She has a Master's degree in Broadcast Journalism from the American University in Washington, DC. Ashwini lives in Singapore with her husband and two sons.